3 43

D1276585

DATE DUE

DATE DUE			
DEC 0 6 1993 S			

WITHDRAWN

A DECADE OF DEFICITS

A DECADE OF DEFICITS

Congressional Thought and Fiscal Action

STEVEN E. SCHIER

State University
of New York
Press

Published by
State University of New York Press, Albany

© 1992 State University of New York

All rights reserved

Printed in the United States of America

No part of this book may be used or reproduced
in any manner whatsoever without written permission
except in the case of brief quotations embodied in
critical articles and reviews.

For information, address State University of New York
Press, State University Plaza, Albany, N.Y., 12246

Library of Congress Cataloging in Publication Data

Schier, Steven E.
    A decade of deficits : congressional thought and fiscal action /
Steven E. Schier.
        p.   cm.
    Includes bibliographical references (p.   ) and index.
    ISBN 0-7914-0955-4 (HC : acid-free) : $47.50. — ISBN
0-7914-0956-2 (PB : acid-free) : $15.95
        1. Budget deficits—United States.   2. Fiscal policy–United
States.   3. United States. Congress.   I. Title.
HJ2052.S337   1992
339.5'23'0973—dc20   91-13464
                                                                CIP

10 9 8 7 6 5 4 3 2 1

CONTENTS

298234

To
Donald S. Schier
and
Richard F. Schier
who showed
me the way

PREFACE

Students of Congress have been known to remark that the public hates Congress but loves their own particular legislators. I find that generalization easy to understand after years of questioning legislators in interviews and reading their public statements. The contradiction was abundantly apparent in the 1980s as fiscal problems created a new policy agenda for Congress. Large and persistent deficits dominated congressional attention. Most lawmakers with whom I met voiced serious concern about the federal deficit and could outline cogently their preferred solution to the problem. When constituents encountered such views in town meetings and personal visits, no doubt they often concluded that their representative or senator had thought long and hard about the problem and advocated a defensible way to reduce it. The problem of chronic fiscal imbalance lies less with individual members of Congress than among them collectively. How to get a majority to agree to even one of the myraid of possible solutions? That was the signal problem of fiscal politics in the 1980s.

Researching and writing this book produced an admiration for many of the legislators I encountered and a deep frustration with the fiscal policy product of their institution since 1980. Given the demands upon their time and attention, lawmakers' level of fiscal understanding, though seldom academically sophisticated, proved to be reasonably sound. Their insights about congressional politics were more acute, based on years of strongly motivated observation. Therein lies a great share of the deficit problem. Any solution first must appeal to lawmakers' political sensibilities that are rooted in the imperative of guarding programs of importance to their constituents or to themselves ideologically. The politics of programs dominates congressional life and became the central topic of floor debate over fiscal policy in the 1980s. Legislators spoke most readily about programs during my interviews. In the absence of realistic fiscal leadership by Presidents Reagan and Bush (until mid-1990), the legislature proved unable to aggregate program preferences into a long-term plan to eliminate deficits. In fiscal politics, the whole of Congress proved to be much less than the sum of its parts.

My heavy reliance upon personal interviews and congressional documents dictated certain features of the book's citation technique. The numerous quotations from lawmakers caused me to not footnote them individually. Instead, Appendix I supplies a list of interviews by name and date, so that the particular source of a quotation can be determined. Some quotations from legislators or staffers are anonymous, pursuant to their preferences. A small number of interviews are not listed in Appendix I because the lawmaker desired total anonymity. Also, all references from the *Congressional Record* are identified in the notes by date and page in order to make them easier to locate.

My thanks go first and foremost to the over one hundred Representatives and Senators who granted me time to discuss fiscal issues with them. Some eighty congressional staff members also graciously consented to talk with me, and a majority of legislative assistants on budget issues kindly completed and returned a questionnaire about their legislator's fiscal views. Without their cooperation, this book could not have been written.

Certain individuals deserve special recognition for their contributions. Guy Clough, formerly a legislative assistant to Senator Nancy Kassebaum (R-Kansas), frequently shared his insights about fiscal politics and the Budget committee and was a source of much sound advice about research strategy. Members of the majority staff of the Senate Budget committee in 1986, particularly David Nummy, also helped enhance the quality of my research. Jim Thurber of the American University found time from his busy schedule to direct the administration of our questionnaire of congressional offices, proving to be a conscientious and convivial coworker. At the Brookings Institution, Paul Peterson and Thomas Mann, his successor as director of governmental studies, supplied me office space, a phone, and library access. Joe White gave me invaluable advice at several stages of my writing. Allen Schick's comments on an early draft of this work aided its quality immensely. Aaron Wildavsky also gave me much needed criticism of my early thinking on this subject. Steve Frantzich and Barbara Hinckley aided me with moral support and useful analysis of earlier drafts. My colleagues at Carleton College, particularly Norman Vig, Gary Wynia, and Michael Zuckert, also aided the conceptual growth of my efforts. Carleton's Dean Roy Elveton twice generously provided research funds.

My research effort yielded far more than just this book. Senator Rudy Boschwitz (R-Minn.) at the conclusion of our interview introduced me to his press secretary, who eventually became my spouse. Our marriage remains a far more satisfying outcome of my work in Washington than any book I could write. Mary improved this study through her thorough knowledge of congressional politics and sharp editorial skills. Above all, her sainted patience permitted me to soldier long hours toward the book's completion. Thanks also go to our daughter, Anna Maria, for putting up with this project during the first two years of her life. She learned forbearance at an early age.

CHAPTER 1

The Argument in Brief

My argument rests on the proposition that the behavior and institutional capacity of Congress is shaped by the thought processes of its members. This generalization is a staple of the congressional literature, but few analysts in recent years have been able to examine in depth the thinking of legislators in Washington.[1] Lawmakers are frequently too busy to bother with lengthy interviews. Yet there is no better way to understand their thinking than to probe it with members directly. This book analyzes the congressional response to the "deficit decade" of the 1980s through a depiction of thought processes articulated by the lawmakers themselves.

Thoughts produce actions, but how are thoughts influenced? Legislators act upon conscious conclusions when deciding how to vote on bills. The knowledge of another actor's preferences and willingness to accede to them is a direct influence upon their voting choices. A lawmaker may respond favorably to a plea from important constituency interests or to the persuasion of a popular president of his or her party, for example. But behavior is also shaped by structuring the available knowledge or alternatives. Fiscal committees first lay the contours of the issue at hand. The House leadership then can manipulate floor procedures to encourage a desired outcome by barring consideration of a popular alternative. Staff and professional analysts as well as the "political stratum" of elite opinion-makers in Washington and the national media may define for legislators the problem to be solved and appropriate means for solving it.[2] This influence is more indirect in that legislators are not necessarily aware of the actions taken to shape their choices, nor do they always take a detached and critical view of the Washington "conventional wisdom" surrounding the votes they must cast. Understanding congressional thinking requires recognition of the influences that legislators do not see as well.

One topic that has occupied congressional thoughts far more

than in previous decades is the budget. Large deficits and the political difficulties trailing in their wake often consumed the legislative agenda. In some sessions during the 1980s, over half of the roll-call votes in both the House and the Senate related to the budget.[3] That fiscal matters dominated the congressional agenda during this time testifies to the importance of budget thinking to institutional behavior. Students of Congress have increased their scrutiny of the budget process correspondingly. Most of these works concerned themselves with explaining how the process operated or the relationships between process and fiscal policy results.[4]

The focus here is a bit different. I explore the policy and political thinking of legislators about budget questions in order to better understand why Congress would undertake major policy departures in 1981 but fail to cope adequately with their consequences in subsequent years. No claim is made to broader explanation of congressional behavior, but this work has its share of implications for decision-making beyond the fiscal policy arena. This chapter introduces a framework for understanding how legislators approach budget issues, presenting general themes that are empirically documented in greater detail later in the book.

First, what are "budget issues"? A broad definition would include most of the consequential legislation Congress passes—budget resolutions, reconciliation, authorization, and appropriation bills. Though all such measures receive attention here, the primary focus concerns budget resolutions and reconciliation bills, because they can set parameters for more specific spending decisions.[5] Resolutions set targets for spending in each of eighteen "functions" or policy categories within the federal budget and specify a minimum level of revenues. Reconciliation bills contain changes in authorization and appropriations levels to enforce the discipline of the resolution. For this reason, John Gilmour terms them a "centerpiece" of the budget process.[6] Aggregative decisions of this sort make possible sweeping fiscal changes, allowing the budget process to serve as a mechanism for Congress to work its will in fiscal policy.

The 1980s witnessed the decline of resolutions and reconciliation as effective disciplines on congressional spending.[7] After an impressive demonstration of these measures' ability to constrain authorizations and appropriations in 1981, Congress began to delay resolutions and reconciliation because it could not decide what to do about fiscal policy in the face of large deficits. The legislature was forced to abandon the "big picture" and scrap instead over the specifics of spending with a recalcitrant White House. The parts of budgeting overwhelmed the problem as a whole. Why did this happen? An explanation will benefit from a thorough study of legislative thinking during this period. A framework of policy thinking on budget issues is identifiable.

All members of the House and Senate, with varying degrees of analytical sophistication, approach budget issues from a perspective encompassing three elements: (1) long-standing conceptions of the proper "role of government" in the economy, involving an "economic ideology" about the appropriate degree of government action in the allocation of public goods, distribution of economic rewards, and stabilization of macroeconomic cycles[8]; (2) a "practical theory" of how the economy works, both nationally and in their constituencies, and how it will perform in the future; and (3) a political estimation of the direction and intensity of the preferences of those who have important effects upon the attainment of member goals—constituents, party leaders, interest groups, colleagues, and the president. Legislators' goals motivate them to work through this framework to a decision on budget measures. Goals are defined here as three: satisfying constituents, making good public policy, and attaining influence within Washington.[9] Members' substantive fiscal convictions, deriving from ideology and practical theories, are an important part of the process of political estimation because they define "good policy."

This "political economy" of legislators encompasses the direct influences upon legislative behavior. As lawmakers confront budget matters, various components of this mental framework become controlling upon behavior, as is noted later in this chapter and in the next. Direct influences on voting operate much as John Kingdon suggested in his earlier work on voting decisions.[10] Indirect influences become important to the extent that they manipulate aspects of members' political economy. For example, the tremulousness of economic analysts and Washington elites over deficits drives lawmakers to worry about stabilization. Committees take the allocative and distributive beliefs of members into account when shaping budget bills. Party leaders do the same when scheduling alternatives for floor vote.

What follows is a schematic overview of legislators' political economy. The framework derives from interviews with 113 Representatives and Senators conducted from 1985 to 1987, and a survey in 1986 of 67 Senate and 253 House legislative assistants concerning their legislators' budget voting and fiscal views.[11] Chapter 2 examines the substantive differences in congressional political economy in more depth.

In discussing political economy, it is first necessary to recall a hoary commonplace about our national legislators. The introductory student of Congress is often told that the institution is representative in both the good and bad senses of that word; that it has its share of saints, sinners, cerebrals, and dolts. So it is with fiscal policy. Some legislators can address this policy area with the sophistication of a professional economist (such as Senator Phil Gramm of Texas and Representative Jim Moody of Wisconsin), while others are hard pressed to articulate views beyond those found in the most banal of partisan discussions. The average legislator occupies a position somewhere between these extremes, that of the educated layperson in fiscal debate. Representatives and Senators are usually quick to indicate the limits of their knowledge ("I'm no economist," many say, usually with an accompanying "Thank God!") and to explain how they arrive at decisions within these limits. Lawmakers' political economy on budget issues is defined by such limits.

ECONOMIC IDEOLOGY

Any ideological construct has a constraining function. It serves to guide an individual in linking "beliefs, whether beliefs about facts or values, and attitudes, defined as predispositions to act in certain ways toward certain sets of objects or events, with behavior."[12] The economic ideology of legislators reveals much about the course of congressional policy decisions in the 1980s. Talk with members in their offices or in cloakrooms, read the floor debates on budget resolutions and reconciliation bills, and the contours of ideology become apparent. Members continually address the three elements of fiscal policy identified some time ago by Richard Mus-grave: allocation, distribution, and stabilization.[13] The particular problems within each of these elements varies across time and among individuals, but fiscal thinking in the institution receives its structure from these ideas.

Allocation is the provision of "public" or "social" goods by the government—that is, the provision of goods that cannot be provided by the market due to a variety of market failures (such as imperfect information or externalities).[14] Though members, ac-cording to James Moody (D-Wis.), an economist, "do not know what these terms mean in the abstract, they do understand them when you explain them, and realize that they deal with these prob-lems all the time." The annual congressional debate about spend-ing priorities in a budget resolution is concerned centrally with matters of allocation. The perennial argument about "guns and butter" involves which public goods deserve allocation and in what amounts. More for defense? For environmental protection? For public works?

A related allocational issue in Congress concerns the overall size of the government in the economy. This is the definition of "allocation" incorporated by Weatherford and McDonnell in their concept of economic ideology.[15] Conservative Democrats and Re-publicans were likely to be preoccupied with whether the national government consumes too large a share of the Gross National Product. Ronald Reagan brought to the budget battles of the 1980s the strong conviction that the size of government was far too large: "When government starts to take more than 25 percent of the economy, that's when the trouble starts. Well, we zoomed above that a long time ago. That's how we got in this economic mess. We can't solve it with more tax and spend."[16] More liberal Democrats did not view this number as a totem, but focused instead, in the words of Representative Major Owens (D-N.Y.), upon "programs and the need to help people, not some meaningless percentage."

A second element of economic ideology is the long-controversial issue of redistribution, or, as labeled by Musgrave and Musgrave, distribution: "The adjustment of the distribution of income and wealth to assure conformance with what society con-siders a fair or just distribution."[17] Democrats in the 1980s made this their theme when they decried the lack of "fairness" in the fiscal approach of the Reagan and Bush administrations. This conviction dovetailed nicely with the political imperative of supporting programs that had the approval of their supporting electoral coalitions back home. In other words, redistributive programs—Social Security foremost among them—constituted a line of battle on which Democrats usually held firm. Republicans after the Reagan rout in 1981 were forced to rhetorically "me too" on this matter. Even the White House in the midst of the 1981 budget battle had to claim that the "safety net" of programs for the "truly needy" would be kept intact. Democrats built strong defensive fortifications on this front. Ideology and politics demanded it.

One avenue of Republican attack that produced some Democratic defections involved the issue of "incentives." Southern Democrats, particularly the members of the Conservative Democratic Forum in the House, resembled Republicans in wanting more incentives in tax and welfare programs. Representative Marvin Leath (D-Tex.), an important budget leader for more conservative Democrats in the 1980s, endorsed a flat tax and fellow budget warrior Charles Stenholm (D-Tex.) argued that his party must become more "incentive- and opportunity-oriented." The problem of rec-onciling the differing attitudes within the Democratic party on allocation and distribution in the face of a popular conservative president produced partisan calamity for Democratic congressional leaders in the early 1980s.[18]

The stable basis of economic ideology in Congress concerns allocation and distribution. These are legislators' core ideological beliefs because they concern particular programs, the substantive building blocks of the legislative process. As a voting record is established, constituents come to identify lawmakers with an allocative and distributive program philosophy. Personally and politically, these two dimensions of ideology anchor most members' fiscal attitudes. Legislators know their colleagues' allocative and distributive views well and can identify them readily.

The most abstruse and variable concern of economic ideology for legislators is that of economic stabilization, "the use of budget policy as a means of providing high employment, a reasonable level of price stability, and an appropriate rate of economic growth."[19] Musgrave's definition suggests active fiscal intervention by government to smooth short-term fluctuations in the economy. Though most Democrats have no problem endorsing such efforts, more conservative legislators object to this sort of budget strategy. They hold, consistent with a minimalist allocation view, that short-term stabilization by government cannot be successful; that limited government is necessary for a vibrant market economy.

But this is an argument over strategy; over what long-term approach to stabilization is best to pursue. Most budget votes in contrast concern tactical—short-term—stabilization questions. Regardless of their theoretical declarations about how to manage the economy, both liberal and conservative legislators cast votes believing that discretionary stabilization policy does matter to them politically. Determining how fiscal choices might alter conditions in the nation and therefore back home is one way to safeguard the economic base of one's district, a prime imperative for lawmakers.[20] The vast majority in Congress in practice treat the budget as a valuable stabilization tool, regardless of their allocative beliefs. The prevalence of this "tactical stabilization consensus" is born of a need to keep the economy thriving and a belief that congressional fiscal decisions make a difference in this.

While this consensus seems a tidy concept, the 1980s produced nothing but confusion about the macroeconomic effects of deficits. Economists and the "political stratum" blamed deficits for inflation, the high dollar, high interest rates, the trade deficits, low market confidence, among other evils. White and Wildavksy note that "while public discourse so often claimed national interest in avoiding the evident evils of deficits, most assertions about how the economy works, including assertions about the deficit, proved inaccurate."[21] Given this cacophony, what was a legislator to do? Most believed some sort of deficit reduction was necessary, but consensus on a number became the big challenge each year. Gramm-Rudman-Hollings reduced the difficulty of the deficit target only slightly, once it became clear Congress would not adhere seriously to the law's targets. Ultimately, the economy provided the answer. No big drop, so no big action by Congress. Such was the practical extent of the congressional stabilization consensus during the 1980s.

Legislators have a clear sense of a "political business cycle"[22] linking the results of economic events and electoral outcomes. This leads them, regardless of their professed economic ideology, to view decisions about fiscal policy in terms of immediate mac-roeconomic impacts. Broader discussions of stabilization strategy do not figure prominently in legislative life. Such topics require members to think big, while their everyday legislative routines mandate that they focus upon specific parts of the fiscal whole. Unlike allocation and distribution, stabilization deals primarily with the budget as an aggregate, not as a collection of specific programs involving particular committee jurisdictions and constit-uent clients. Given their committee and electoral concerns, legisla-tors tend to be more program- than aggregate-oriented about bud-geting.[23] The "gut" issues of budgeting do not concern esoterica such as Keynesian versus monetarist interpretations of fiscal policy. Rather they involve the conflict resulting when allocation and dis-tribution preferences do not comport with the simple tactical im-perative of deficit reduction. As Jim Moody (D-Wis.) put it: "At the core of the deficit issue are gut-wrenching political decisions. Only rudimentary ideas about our general fiscal direction are nec-essary to solve it."

Inevitably in budgeting, tensions develop between particular elements of a legislator's economic ideology, forcing members to contemplate the consistency of their stabilization, distribution, and allocation goals. New deficit reduction imperatives caused conflict between stabilization desires and both the allocational and dis-tributional ends of lawmakers. The discomfort for legislators grew more acute because the electoral and substantive justifications for program concerns clashed with a signal problem for the "political stratum"—the overall deficit. These cross pressures explain much of the congressional muddle as the deficits grew during the first half of the decade.[24]

PRACTICAL THEORIES

Authority over fiscal policy requires that legislators comprehend the reasons for economic events. A particular budget must be con-sidered in terms of its immediate cyclical impact, and this necessi-tates understanding what is transpiring in the economy. Con-gressional decisions turn upon the quality of economic prognostication. What will economic conditions be during the year when this budget is in place? Answers rest upon legislators' premises concerning the nature and origin of current economic conditions.

A steady stream of information flows to members about the economy.[25] What would motivate a legislator to clarify one's theories? All shared the need to be able to prepare a brief explanation for constituent consumption. Specialists on the fiscal committees (Ways and Means, Finance, Appropriations, and Budget) had to follow the economy more carefully to be on top of their jobs. But even they could rely heavily on staff for analysis, beyond whatever explanations would suffice for constituent consumption. Ultimately, the only members who monitor the economy analytically are those who bring adequate intellectual equipment with them when they are sworn into office. Representative Willis Gradison (R-Ohio), one such member (Harvard MBA), commented that "you really have to rely upon your intellectual capital once you get here. You just don't have time to learn that many new concepts and mental approaches. If you don't come here with the intellectual resources, you usually have to rely on others to furnish them for you."

The economy back home is the focus of the most extensively contemplated "practical theory" in the minds of lawmakers. Members have a detailed exposure to district conditions and an occupational motivation to track them that simply outstrips their concern and knowledge about national trends. This is not to say that they are ignorant about national conditions, or that their simplifications concerning them are inappropriate for the decisions they must make. During a decade when most of the conventional wisdom about deficits turned out to be wrong, knowledge of the economy did not necessarily help legislators to do the right thing.

The substance of budget debates encompasses economic predictions alongside ideological argumentation that primarily concerns questions of program priorities: How much for defense, Medicare, environmental protection, the poor? Representative Ralph Regula (R-Ohio) explained the emphasis on program spending: "Because we have a micro, micro, micro focus in Congress. We are used to dealing with programs. That's what we work with. The big picture dissolves into a budget of smaller concerns." Regula supplies an important explanation for the decline of "big picture" aggregate measures like resolutions and reconciliation during the

course of the decade. As the economy perked along, program defense intensified, making deficit politics intractable. Gramm-
Rudman-Hollings was born out of the frustration resulting from
just this tendency.[26]

POLITICAL INFLUENCES

Given that complex voting situations occur frequently in congressional budgeting, what role do other sorts of influences—such as
the political pressures of constituents, president, and interest
groups—play in choices on the floor? They are a staple of much
political science research on congressional voting,[27] and represent
the foundation of a model of behavior accepted by many students
of the legislature, identified by Arthur Maass as "partisan mutual
adjustment."[28] In this framework, Congress is understood as primarily performing the function of aggregating "particular interests" and "coordinating through partisan mutual adjustment the
opinions that have been articulated by others in support of their
particular interests."[29] This conception directs attention away
from the substantive concerns of legislators in order to generalize
about the process by which decisions are made.

A complete picture of Congress and budget-making in the
1980s requires acknowledgment that legislators do evidence serious concern with the "common good."[30] The question regarding
budget decision-making is, when? Most of the remainder of this
book is devoted to an answer. I begin by considering how policy is
important when legislators vote on the budget.

Admittedly the sort of pure politics of partisan mutual adjustment occurs at times in budget voting, but policy concerns are
central both in explaining budget voting and understanding the
onset of the deficit problem.[31] The task then is to fit "partisan
mutual adjustment" into the context of budget decision-making.
Political influences do affect both the weighting and substance of
ideology and practical theories in budget resolution and reconciliation votes. On the "philosophical votes"—budget resolutions—
their influence tends to be indirect; a lawmaker's general ideological orientation tends to control the choice. In more program-
specific reconciliation and appropriations voting, though, political
influences tend to have more pronounced effects upon decisions.

Perhaps the best way to examine the political influences on resolution, reconciliation, and appropriations voting is to consider them in terms of John Kingdon's formulation of the "field of forces" in the mind of a legislator deciding how to vote.[32] The most important force in this "field" on resolution votes is that of personal convictions, as will be noted more fully in the next chapter.[33] Fully 95 percent of the nonspecialist legislators I interviewed about their resolution vote in 1986 mentioned that personal convictions were highly important in helping them to make up their minds.[34] These convictions include both economic ideology and practical theories about the economy.[35]

When are particular interests most likely to succeed in finding a receptive audience among legislators? Reconciliation and appropriations bills are the venue for lawmakers to service these needs.[36] Members commonly distinguished between the overall vote that is involved in a budget resolution and the "real teeth of the budget process," as Senator William Proxmire (D-Wis.) put it, the reconciliation bill.[37] After 1981 the teeth lost much of their bite. Reconciliation was used only to increase revenues or reduce entitlement spending to reduce the deficit at the margin. The 1990 deficit reduction compromise, which at long last promised more than marginal reductions in red ink, likewise relied mainly on entitlement cuts and tax increases. Allen Schick notes that for most of the 1980s, reconciliation bills were vehicles for all sorts of extraneous program-related legislation.[38] In reconciliation and appropriations bills, according to Rep. Bill Richardson, (D-N. Mex.): "the whole situation is more political. You deal with issues of spending that are not dealt with elsewhere and you get your shots at saving your programs. I tend to look at it more in terms of narrow self-interest." Other legislators mentioned them as opportunities to "help out your programs," "to do some good for your own priorities," and the like.

Certain durable relationships between legislator attitudes and political influences are evident throughout the tumult of budgeting in the 1980s. Figure 1.1 introduces these relationships, with elaboration in depth to follow in the next chapter. Legislators have ideological and political reasons for supporting particular programs, leading them to emphasize some parts of the budget over others. Much of this motivation is rooted in their constituency,

FIGURE 1.1   Electoral Influences upon
Congressional Fiscal Thinking

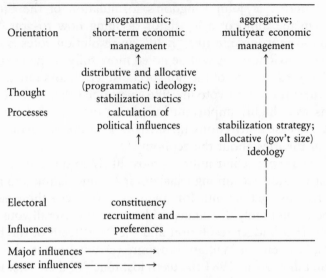

Orientation	programmatic; short-term economic management	aggregative; multiyear economic management
	↑	↑
Thought	distributive and allocative (programmatic) ideology; stabilization tactics	
Processes	calculation of political influences	
	↑	stabilization strategy; allocative (gov't size) ideology
		↑
Electoral	constituency	
Influences	recruitment and — — — — — —⌐ preferences	

Major influences ⎯⎯⎯⎯⎯→
Lesser influences — — — — —→

producing a strong and consistent pull in given programmatic directions. Stabilization tactics—attempts to manage the economy for prosperity and electoral reward in the short term—also are influenced strongly by the fear of electoral reprisal back home. Concern with the fiscal situation as a whole, in contrast, involves more long-term stabilization strategies and, to a lesser extent, "macroallocation" (size of government), as well as practical theories about the course of the economy. Constituency recruitment plays a less prominent role in the formulation of strategic stabilization theories. Legislative views on these matters can be shaped much more by the "political stratum"—Washington policy circles and the national media—that reflects their opinions.

The story of the 1980s in congressional budgeting is, in terms of the diagram, that of the primacy of the programmatic over the aggregative orientation. More precisely, the cheerleaders for the aggregative orientation demanded improvement in the deficit, placing some overall constraint upon the usually central programmatic motivations of lawmakers. As the media and economists cried wolf, Congress felt it had to respond.[39] But as the economy persisted in growth after 1982, the real economic pressure for action was not so great. This permitted lawmakers to rationalize their inability to reduce the deficit, as will be explored in the following chapter. Only extreme economic duress or strong fiscal offensives by popular presidents—Reagan in 1981, Bush in 1990—could dislodge the primacy of programs.

MEMBER GOALS

The role of political influences in budget voting becomes clearer when they are related to lawmakers' goals. Richard Fenno discovered three goals among the members of Congress: making good public policy, satisfying constituents, and gaining intra-Washington influence.[40] Chapter 2 notes that most legislators named personal policy convictions as the major goal they pursued in voting on budget resolutions. But this general statement masks a series of calculations. Satisfying Fenno's three goals is not a mutually exclusive proposition; one can achieve much with one vote.

Most of the budget votes of the 1980s involved trying to avoid offending constituents by voting for the best available alternative. As Representative Doug Walgren (D-Pa.) put it: "So many of these votes are exercises in damage control. You don't like what you see and just have to look for the one that hurts you the least back home and that you personally can live with." Legislators had some room for maneuver because any single budget vote would not be of high salience to constituents. None of the legislators I spoke with, for example, indicated that their vote on the budget resolution in 1986 attracted significant interest in their constituencies. But a string of votes offensive to one's supporting electoral coalition programmatically or in the aggregate threatened electoral danger, as Kingdon found in 1970.[41]

Conflicts involving the constituency do occur, though. A legislator can be torn between supporting an overall budget measure and defending a particular part of the budget important back home. Composing a successful resolution, reconciliation, or appropriations bill became largely a matter of muting or avoiding enough of these tensions so as to gain the support of a majority of legislators. Reconciliation and appropriations politics involved this far more because they entailed actual cuts, not just overall targets. By the mid-1980s, majorities were cultivated through proposals that claimed to hit every important budget claimant "fairly." This strategy was a response to the preference members often heard from constituents to "take their fair share of cuts if others have to as well." The "fair share" received specific definition in reconciliation bills, leading to intense negotiations and more interest-based activity. The definition in practice seldom provided for equal sacrifice and by mid-decade, the scope of reconciliation bills had narrowed so that cuts affected only a few claimants. In fact, different primary victims suffered in different years. In 1981 the working poor and state and local governments due to budget cuts, in 1982 and 1984 business via revenue increases, and from 1986 to 1988 the military through real spending freezes. Each could be stigmatized either for wasteful spending or unnecessary tax favors. Only in 1990 did a large deficit reduction package pass that required considerable sacrifice from a large number of budget claimants.

The pursuit of intra-Washington influence is of small importance in budget voting. Why not use a budget vote to curry favor with other power centers, such as the party leadership and the president? Neither of them usually were all that effective as power centers in budget politics. From 1982 to 1989 the president usually performed a negative role of keeping certain items off the deficit reduction agenda. In 1990 George Bush's demands for unpopular deficit reduction measures caused many even in his own party to distance themselves from him. Party leaders throughout the decade had few rewards and punishments to employ with their followers. More importantly, few lawmakers viewed resolution and reconciliation votes as opportunities for horse-trading one's way to power within Congress. Instead, they commonly referred to them as "exercises in philosophy" and "serious attempts at deficit reduction," policy reasons indeed. Of course, a certain amount of bargaining occurs in the budget process, particularly on the specific provisions of reconciliation bills, and appropriations politics involved much dealing over programs. But this usually concerned policy and constituency goals, not a desire to please those prominent in Washington. Voting to satisfy D.C. luminaries may occur, but it is not at all common.[42]

THE INSTITUTIONAL ENVIRONMENT

This is not to say the Washington environment has no say in budget outcomes. The party leadership, fiscal committees, and conventional wisdom of Washington constitute three important but indirect influences from that environment. Party leaders throughout the 1980s influenced the composition of resolution, reconciliation, and appropriations bills in order to facilitate passage by their chamber. As one House leadership staffer indicated: "We can influence the framing of alternatives, more so on budget resolutions in the Budget committee than on reconciliation and appropriations, which come more from the committees themselves. But we can influence at the margin and also set up a rule to help our alternative to prevail. We do this a lot." In the Senate similar efforts are attempted, though the "informal nature of floor proceedings gets in our way somewhat," according to a Democratic leadership staffer. Budget, Appropriations, and tax committee members keep the floor in mind as well. Legislators from all such committees talked of "getting it passed" and "keeping your eye on the floor" when formulating bills. But the committees do compose the product, framing choice within the floor constraints they perceive. Legislators may claim to follow only convictions in floor voting, but committees do much necessary agenda-narrowing work of independent substantive importance to the bills voted upon on the floor. The specialists define the issue with some sense of the convictions of their nonspecialist peers in mind.

The Washington media and various economists could be counted upon throughout the decade to press the case for deficit reduction. Practically every economic evil was at one point blamed on deficits. The deficit also came to be viewed as a moral evil, as an example of a Congress that could not govern. As Democratic Representative Marvin Leath claimed: "We get hit over the head by this all the time. In the media. We are cowards and can't govern and the economy is going to go to hell. How can you not pay attention to all this?" Personal convictions, the fulcrum of budget voting, are so shaped.

If this sort of hectoring wasn't enough, four other reasons made budget votes high salience decisions for legislators. First, resolution, reconciliation, and appropriations votes directly concern one of the "great issues" of the time, that of chronically large deficits. The "macro" policy stakes are sizeable to most lawmakers. Second, budget issues are the subject of "high politics" between the legislative and executive branches.[43] The political arena for these issues is of grand scale. Third, decisions made on resolutions and reconciliation bills shape the range of choices available for lawmakers on their authorizing and appropriation committees. The consequences for their everyday worklives are substantial. Fourth, parts of the constituency may well question any budget vote. An explanation must be prepared for home consumption.

All this explains why budget issues seriously concern every member of Congress. It also indicates why the norm of specialization does not play a large role in the consideration of budget resolutions and reconciliation bills. The Budget committees are not viewed as founts of expertise and political influence. During much of their existence they have had to fight jurisdictional battles with both appropriations and authorizing committees.[44] Budget committee members may disseminate information to their colleagues, but seldom exercise political influence over them. As one Democratic representative stated: "Lord, a budget resolution isn't like some technical appropriations bill. On those you have to rely on the subcommittee members to explain what's in it, and maybe get a hint on how to vote. There are all sorts of sources of information on a budget resolution, and most of us have firm views on it that will guide our choices." Representative Jim Slattery (D-Kan.), a member of the Budget committee, put it this way: "We provide information and try to sell our proposal to our colleagues, but we don't direct anybody's voting. That's a matter of personal convictions."

This weak specialization norm, combined with the high salience of budget votes, produced a policy formulation process in the 1980s involving many effective participants and decision-making units. Resolution construction involved consultation with members of the majority party in the House and Senate, and the party leader role became one of "brokering" among the various perspectives involved in the process.[45] Authorizing committees, with the exception of 1981, wrote the specific language in reconciliation bills. Another set of players—the large Appropriations committees and their subcommittees—put together spending legislation in the form of particular appropriations bills or, more frequently later in the decade, composite "continuing resolutions." Because members voted their own convictions on the floor, alignments were volatile and outcomes unpredictable, producing difficulties for the budget process timetable. Much of the remainder of this book analyzes such troubles.

The political economy of legislators demonstrates the importance of parts over the whole; of programs over aggregates; of allocation and distribution over stabilization. From the minds of legislators come the limits of institutional capacity on fiscal matters. They are severe, as following chapters will illustrate, making the budget revolution of 1981 and the deficit reduction of 1990 seem all that more remarkable. A more thorough exploration of the substance of legislators' political economy in the next chapter will cultivate our appreciation of the extraordinary events discussed in chapter 3.

CHAPTER 2

The Political Economy of Legislators

Political economy is a complex concept encompassing ideological convictions, empirical policy assessments, and political calculations. Political science has examined all of these aspects of legislative behavior separately, often in great detail.[1] All are evident when legislators decide on budget issues. This chapter first presents a snapshot of congressional political economy in the 1980s. What were the ideological divisions, practical theories, and political assessments among lawmakers during this time? A depiction of all this will inform a discussion of the major budget events of the decade in ensuing chapters.

Secondly, I examine how lawmakers personally handled the stress that deficit politics produced. They endured personal tension throughout the decade between their desire to preserve individual programs (microallocative and distributive preferences) and the perceived need to "be responsible" and reduce the deficit substantially. In the parlance of social psychology, lawmakers encountered cognitive dissonance, defined by Leon Festinger as when the "obverse" of one mental element "would follow from the other."[2] That is, voting for budget bills that defended programs or held taxes down usually meant endorsing large deficits in practice. What rationalizations could lessen the tension over seemingly contradictory behavior? The arguments legislators voiced on this point reveals how they managed to respect themselves in the midst of a potentially frightful inconsistency, permitting Congress to perpetuate deficits throughout the decade.

A NOTE ON METHOD

Access to legislators is not what it used to be, but my meetings with over one hundred legislators taught me much about their thinking. It also revealed to me the problems of using a strict question schedule with elite interviews. The statements of members usually did not conform to tidy and discrete categories as I had hoped they might. Responses were variable enough that in many instances a coherent coding of them was not possible. Unlike John Kingdon, who followed a brief schedule concerned with influences on particular votes, my questions were often broad-ranging and required complex and lengthy responses. Also, unlike Kingdon, I could not get in to see legislators right after they voted, but rather only when it was convenient for them. All this led me to make my primary emphasis that of recording the broader contours of congressional political economy. These can be identified clearly, and certain correlations duly noted, as can the implications of this thinking for the fiscal record of Congress in the 1980s.

What follows is a depiction of each aspect of congressional political economy through analysis of a questionnaire of House and Senate offices in 1986 and my own elite interviews with seventy Representatives who were not specialists on budget issues.[3] Details on the questions asked and the method of the questionnaire can be found in the Appendixes.[4] The consistency of my interview findings with the questionnaire results supports the reliability of the questionnaire data. The survey asked both general questions about economic attitudes and specifically about influences on the vote for the budget resolution in 1986. Some context on the budget politics in that year is necessary in interpreting the data that follows.

THE 1986 RESOLUTION

The FY 1987 budget resolution arrived in the middle of a decade of deficit politics and was the first after the passage of Gramm-Rudman-Hollings (GRH), which mandated a solution to the fiscal problem via deficit targets that would be enforced by the threat of mandatory across-the-board deficit cuts. By then, habits of thought about chronic deficits and their consequences were well-entrenched. As Rep. Matt McHugh (D-N.Y.) said at the time: "Members have been facing the same music for four years now. Always the deficit is too big, the economy may reverse any day, and we can't get agreement with the White House on a package. Those basics remain the same in 1986."

Senate Republicans, still in the majority, were forced to take the lead in the process, given that the Democratic House and Reagan remained at a virtual standoff on solving the fiscal imbalance. After lengthy Budget committee hearings and several floor amendments, a resolution passed with substantial bipartisan support and White House opposition. Despite employing relatively realistic economic assumptions from the Congressional Budget Office (unlike many previous resolutions of the decade), it still managed to hit the GRH target of a $144 billion deficit.[5] Domestic spending was not greatly altered, but the resolution did call for $45 billion in additional revenue over three years. The vote on final passage was 70–25, with certain strong liberals and conservatives voting in opposition.

The House, however, did not respond to the offer of "political protection" included in the Senate resolution—namely, the inclusion of higher taxes. Speaker O'Neill, in close consultation with Budget chair Bill Gray (D-Pa.), refused to sanction higher revenues unless House Republicans joined in the call. When that was not forthcoming, Gray built consensus around a Democratic package in the Budget committee. His plan cleverly did not call for any more revenues than had the White House. It did lower domestic spending by 2.5 percent below that of the previous year while exempting low-income and children's programs. The really strong medicine was a freeze of defense at the previous year's level, some $16 billion below the Senate resolution. Social Security, as in the Senate plan, was not touched, and CBO assumptions were employed. The House committee passed the resolution 21–7 on May 8 and the full House approved it 245–179, largely along party lines.

The ease with which the resolution passed each chamber suggests that resolutions by 1986 were losing their significance in the budget process.[6] The game now concerned the possibility of GRH cuts, and the budget resolution was merely a dull opening act before the inevitable budget negotiations necessary to reach that year's $144 billion target. Each chamber employed its own strategy to push the president toward taxes. The Senate claimed they were unavoidable, and the House staked out an aggressive bargaining position by slashing defense. This sort of political game of chicken was possible early in the process, when no money was actually on the line.

Accompanying such tactical games among the Senate, House, and president was the long-standing environment of budget politics, involving the turf wars of the various fiscal committees (by then largely won by the tax and appropriations committees at the expense of the Budget committees) and the economic convictions of individual members. The following data illustrate the political economy of members that set the context for the budget games just described. Coalitions are built, after all, from the thoughts of those one seeks to persuade.

CONTOURS OF IDEOLOGY

An appropriate grouping of the House and Senate involves three factions: northern Democrats, southern Democrats, and Republicans. The budget wars of the early 1980s featured each of the three as prominent groupings. Most northern Democrats fought the White House consistently over fiscal priorities. Southern Democrats swung toward Reagan in 1981 but away from him after 1982. Republicans found themselves between the administration and the other party on many issues, opposed to deficits but opposed to taxes and large domestic spending cuts as well.[7] Organizing the data analysis according to these groups relates it to the major battle lines. Further, a more precise analysis by seniority, region, and committee status (member of a fiscal committee or not) yielded no significant differences among members.[8] The above three groups are most empirically meaningful for our analysis as well as the ones most apparent to chroniclers of the process. The coincidence seems hardly incidental.

One is struck immediately in Table 2–1 by the sharp split between southern and other Democrats over stabilization strategy—specifically, over annual budget balance. It was, in fact, this very division that drove southern Democratic "Boll Weevils" in the House into Ronald Reagan's arms in 1981. The president first sent up large spending cuts and decried deficits. Weevils, responding to a clamor from home and to their own ideological

TABLE 2–1   Economic Ideology in Congress in 1986[1]

	Percentage	House (N = 253)			Senate (N = 67)		
		Northern Dem.	Southern Dem.	Republican	Northern Dem.	Southern Dem.	Republican
Balance budget every year	Y	27	66	86	22	63	71
	N	60	24	6	74	38	20
Reduce inequality	Y	64	43	11	73	75	21
	N	16	37	77	14	13	42
Gov't. & GNP too large	Y	37	55	91	26	38	75
	N	40	5	2	48	13	8
Freeze defense	Y	91	70	40	78	86	25
	N	4	23	50	9	14	69
Increase revenues	Y	77	73	18	91	100	44
	N	14	14	69	5	—	42

[1]All entries are percentages of the group listed at the top of each column. Comparisons among the three party/regional groups on each question were all significant at the .05 level. Numbers do not always sum to 100% due to blank or "don't know" responses.

inclinations, approved the president's cuts (known as Gramm-Latta I).[9] By 1986, however, many Weevils had put distance between themselves and the White House. "We were always skeptical of supply-side economics," recalled Marvin Leath (D-Tex.), "and less keen on the big tax cut than on the budget cuts. Once we got the big deficits and the White House failed to propose any feasible solution to them, we parted company." The Weevils' consensus on stabilization lay between liberal Democrats and supply-side Republicans.[10]

Leath, like all lawmakers interviewed, could articulate a rudimentary set of stabilization tactics when asked to identify under what conditions deficits are tolerable. Almost all in Congress will allow them in wartime, and most during a "serious economic emergency." Members of both parties also accept the reality of countercyclical policy as embodied in automatic stabilizers such as unemployment compensation. Consider this exchange between two conservative members of the House in 1985 about the cyclical impact of Gramm-Rudman-Hollings:

> MR. ROEMER (D-La.): If the gentleman would yield further, the gentleman would agree that if the economy were, in fact, showing negative growth, that we would not want to take a $35 billion or $40 billion reduction in spending on top of that negative growth? I just want to make sure that your instructions do not guarantee that we run counter to good common economic sense.
>
> MR. LOTT (R-Miss.): That is correct.[11]

Conservative Republicans and Democrats accept such stabilization tactics as a practical political matter, but do not necessarily endorse countercyclical spending as a theoretically defensible stabilization strategy. This probably explains the split evident in Table 2–1 within Democratic ranks over budget balance as a general goal. Representative Vin Weber (R-Minn.) voiced a widespread conservative skepticism when he claimed that "in endorsing deficit spending during a recession, I am not endorsing Keynesian countercyclical financing as an effective way to economic growth. Other means are preferable. Programs instead automatically kick in, but that is good, because we have to allow this spending in order to help people." This contrasts with the advocacy of Keynesian "pump priming" by many (nonsouthern) Democrats, like Representative Richard Durbin (D.-Ill.): "We should use the budget to stimulate the economy during downturns by creating jobs and undertaking the necessary spending to reduce hardships. By stimulating consumption by the victims of a downturn, we can stimulate economic growth. The question really is: Who should lead our growth? The spending of the wealthy or of the working class and poor? Most Democrats favor the latter."

Lawmakers do not extensively contemplate stabilization actions beyond their immediate economic impact; broader discussions of stabilization strategy do not figure prominently in legislative life. The topic involves the intricacies of applied fiscal policy, an area akin to a committee specialization in the minds of legislators. They are the sorts of questions that members of the "economic" or "fiscal" committees (Banking, Appropriations, Finance, Ways and Means, Budget, and Joint Economic) have thought about the most. One forum where members demonstrate interest and concern with stabilization issues is the hearings of the Budget committees. Economists are regularly called, in an ideologically balanced array, in order to forecast the course of the economy and prescribe fiscal policy. Committee members receive training in the basics of stabilization by questioning witnesses.[12] Aside from similar hearings held occasionally by the tax, Banking, and Appropriations committees of the two chambers, and the Joint Economic committee, stabilization questions receive scant detailed attention. Individual legislators who care little about economic theory seldom are challenged to publicly address such issues, even if they are on a committee holding hearings about them.

By the cyclical logic of stabilization tactics, large deficits grew less defensible as an economic recovery continued through the 1980s. Congress, at the behest of the political stratum, then found a simple prescription to help them avoid the confusions of economists over fiscal policy: the deficit should be reduced. As a policy imperative, it proved to be too simple for practical use; important strategic questions trailed in its wake. To what level, and over what period of time? This question tormented Congress such that by 1985 it passed the Gramm-Rudman-Hollings law establishing binding deficit reduction targets. Even then, debate over the appropriate targets did not disappear, because the tactical challenge of annually meeting them remained politically difficult. The 1990 deficit reduction grew from a specific deficit reduction target set by the president, and agreed to by the congressional leadership, of $500 billion over five years. The legislative debate demonstrated no grand consensus in favor of this amount, but lawmakers resigned themselves to the presidential target and mainly focused on how to assemble the package. Stabilization dominated actual congressional discussion only in 1981, and then only because a popular president pressed a novel fiscal theory. Agreement on stabilization proved elusive in Congress much of the time after 1981 because lawmakers were more concerned with budget parts.

Stabilization questions became so intractable in the 1980s because of their distributive implications for the two parties. Most Democrats tend to favor a countercyclical budget policy that makes redistribution an ongoing achievement of stabilization. The Republican alternative based its growth hopes upon the supply-side effects of reductions in personal marginal income tax rates. As chapter 3 indicates, the congressional conception of supply-side promised salutary short-term stabilization effects and fruition of the right's long-held allocation goal of smaller government. In this way conservatives could avoid the problem of colliding allocation beliefs (limit government) and stabilization tactics (support countercyclical spending). Redistribution did not figure into the plan.

The new supply-side wrinkle illustrates how congressional stabilization thinking shifted more freely in the 1980s than did members' other economic views and political perceptions. What seemed a theoretical revolution in 1981—the triumph of supply-side economics—was soon forgotten in the legislative halls. Battles over economic ideology during the decade centered much more on program-based issues of allocation and distribution than macroeconomic management. Macroeconomic theories and their stabilization strategies do not constitute what might be called the "mundane perspective" of the everyday legislator. Program concerns, politically-based stabilization tactics, and the practical consequences of budget votes do, serving as a sort of ballast against institutional waywardness in the pursuit of economic theories. Such concerns also limit the range of possible solutions to fiscal problems.

The record of Congress in the 1980s is replete with references to the tension between program needs and budget aggregates. In 1985, for example, Senator Joseph Biden (D-Del.) publicly declared that many in his party, including himself, were now "more concerned about the deficit, very bluntly, than we are about the poor."[13] Representative Bill Dickinson (R-Ala.), ranking minority member of the Armed Services committee, explained his opposition to final passage of Gramm-Rudman-Hollings as deriving from this tension:

> Mr. Speaker, I guess this is probably one of the toughest votes that I have had in the twenty years I have been in Congress. Anyone who reviews my voting record would know that I have consistently voted for cuts, against tax increases, and for a strong defense. . . . I want to make cuts, but do not agree with the formula. I think a disproportionate share falls on readiness and defense.[14]

Dickinson's problem involved a conflict between his views on a part and the whole of a budget proposal. Most allocation and distribution issues deal with particular parts of the budget, but stabilization remains an overall imperative.

Table 2–1 also reveals narrow differences between northern and southern House Democrats on distribution; only Republicans strongly opposed redistribution. Senate Democrats were more unified, but also were in the minority in 1986. This meant that no clear majority sentiment could be found in support of any departure from stasis—the White House would prevent efforts at enhancing progressivity through increased taxes on the wealthy (witness the tax reform passed later in 1986), and the votes were not there in the House or Senate (after Democrats again took control in 1987) for a substantial retreat from distributive commitments.

An important rhetorical weapon for Democrats in standing their ground on distribution was the concept of "fairness." Consider this attack by Leon Panetta (D-Cal.) upon Office of Management and Budget (OMB) director David Stockman at a 1983 Budget committee hearing: "Where is the fairness here? How do you defend a budget that increases defense by almost 14 percent and cuts most of the means-tested programs by almost 19 percent. . . . Is that fair?"[15] Panetta and many of his fellow partisans in budget battles were committed to the "protection of the middle class and the poor," in the words of Senator Carl Levin (D-Mich.). This involved (1) preserving certain domestic social programs from further cuts, both those aimed at low-income individuals, such as food stamps, Head Start, and Women's Infants' and Children's feeding program (WIC), and others with middle-class beneficiaries, including student loans and agricultural price supports, and (2) efforts to make income taxes more progressive and increase corporate taxation. In 1983 House Democrats proposed capping benefits from the third year of the Reagan income tax cut at $700, in order to concentrate benefits among lower and middle income individuals and to reduce the deficit. Proposals of this sort stemmed from ideological commitments that Democratic legislators, with the exception of some conservatives, voiced freely in interviews and during floor debate.

One totem for many of them was a graduated income tax system allowing few exclusions so that those with higher incomes would pay a higher percentage in taxes. This preference figured prominently in the tax debates of the decade. The sweeping 1986 tax reform shut down many tax shelters; Senator George Mitchell (D-Me.) led a fight on the Senate floor to include a steeper marginal tax rate for higher income individuals. The 1990 deficit reduction battle with the Bush administration over "taxing the rich" was politically the most successful such Democratic offensive. Another aspect of Democratic "fairness" involved defense of the welfare function of the federal government, a role frequently questioned by Republican conservatives ("the less federal role, the better," one indicated). Beyond the desire for a substantial federal involvement, however, by the mid 1980s Democrats varied considerably on whether basic reform of the welfare system was necessary.[16] Most tended to support federal income maintenance for those of low income, but the problem of incentive effects and the possibility of a work requirement tended to complicate the issue for many. Such concerns prompted Congress to pass a welfare reform in 1988 requiring welfare (AFDC) recipients to sign up for mandatory job training.[17]

Some Republicans identified this preoccupation with incentives as evidence of an ideological victory in congressional battles over the form of redistribution. "We're all supply-siders now," claimed Representative John Hiler (R-Ind.), "The concern with incentive effects in welfare and taxation is a big change from the seventies. We are now more concerned with individual opportunities than with mass entitlements." The mainstream Republican approach directed skepticism at the efficacy of governmental re-distribution and placed heavy emphasis on the effects of taxes and welfare upon individuals. Representative Gene Chappie (R-Cal.), for example, argued that the progressive income tax "penalizes success. The more successful you are, the more it proportionally costs you." Therefore, "nothing could be fairer than to have a common flat percentage across the board." Support for the concept of a flat tax was widespread in Republican circles, and influenced the 1986 tax reform that reduced federal marginal income tax rates to three levels—15, 28, and 33 percent. As Table 2–1 suggests, many southern Democrats in the House, particularly the members of the Conservative Democratic Forum, resembled Republicans in this respect.

A similar pattern is evident in Table 2-·1 on the issue of the size of government, or macroallocation. As progressivity was a totem for many Democrats, so was "percentage of GNP consumed by the national government" for many Republicans, particularly given the trend of the decade. To their distress, the trend was gradually upward in the 1980s—the percentage spurted from 20.6 in 1979 to 24.3 in 1983, before declining somewhat to 22.4 by 1988. One member of the House Republican leadership described the divisions on this within his party: "some moderates are more interested in specific spending programs and not in the overall size of government, but the hard-line conservatives in our party are much more likely to see the need of reducing the percentage of GNP consumed by government as a desirable goal." Few such moderates could be found in GOP ranks in the 1980s, and rhetorically, most Republicans and conservative Democrats found the percentage issue irresistible.

Consider the following examples. Representative James Collins (R-Tex.) in 1981: "Very simply, our nation is stagnant because of too much government. The Democrat budget of the Carter administration called for spending that represented 23 percent of GNP. Policies like this are intolerable."[18] Senator Orrin Hatch (R-Utah) in 1983: "Federal spending has increased from below 20 percent to now 25.7, going on to 26 percent, the highest in the history of this country in modern times. I do not think that is the way to help the country; I do not think it is the way to have a viable economy. I know it is not the way to a high-growth path."[19] Senator Edward

Zorinsky (D-Neb.) in 1985: "As of 1984, the federal government spent almost 25 percent of this nation's GNP. The American people have said 'Enough!' the federal government has to make do with what it has."[20] Why this concern? Representative Howard Neilson, a conservative Republican from Utah, summed up several of the reasons: "Historically, we were able to stay at around 20 percent for a couple of decades, before we started moving upward in the eighties. This is a bad trend, because the more money the government takes, the less money is available for economic transactions, and therefore the less well the economy functions."[21]

Less conservative members took issue with this view of allocation. Representative Matt McHugh (D-N.Y.), a former chair of the Democratic Study Group: "I have a hard time finding a magic number concerning this. I come at it the other way: what are our problems? What problems in our national community must be resolved? There are many problems that the national government must deal with because no one else can do it effectively." Liberal Democrats, long the stewards of activist government, argued it should be judged in terms of necessary tasks rather than overall size.

Allocation involves both a "micro" and "macro" dimension: the specific forms of program expenditure and overall scale of national government spending.[22] Members have well-developed views about program spending, with the substantive divisions ranging from minimal to expanded allocation by the national government. Democrats tend to cluster loosely at the activist pole and Republicans more tightly around the minimalist pole. Representative Don Pease (D-Ohio), for example, is an allocational activist: "It is not inappropriate for government to provide a variety of services. We should decide these on a pragmatic basis by determining whether we can do it better than the private sector. A large number of activities we can do better: national defense, job retraining, foreign policy, education, rural electrification, farm loans." Contrast that with the minimalist approach of Representative Phil Crane (R-Ill.): "The basic role of the national government is to provide defense of the country, diplomacy, administration of justice, and a treasury function. Anything beyond that is subject to challenge." As Crane suggested, the minimalist position usually accords a higher priority to defense spending.

Table 2–1 reveals that it was consensus on the specifics of tax policy and spending programs that allowed Democrats to unify behind a budget resolution in 1986 despite (in the House) clear differences over stabilization strategy. By this time, enough Democrats had become convinced that only by freezing defense and increasing revenues could a solution to the deficit problem be achieved. The broader theoretical differences could be set aside— on size of government, stabilization strategy, and redistribution. Chalk it up to group learning, facilitated by multiple choice budget option exercises distributed in the House by Budget chair James Jones (1981–85), the sheer political danger of altering an entrenched party commitment on Social Security and anger with stubborn presidential resolve to avoid new taxes. As Representative Charles Stenholm (D-Tex.), a staunch conservative, said in 1986: "We disagree on all sorts of the big questions on our party but we do agree on this. The deficit is a problem. Defense and taxes are part of a solution." One need not agree on ideology to agree on programs, or how would so many bills pass?

FIGURING OUT THE ECONOMY

Table 2–2 indicates that by 1986 most members of Congress had thoroughly absorbed the conventional wisdom of the political stratum about deficits. It held that the deficit loomed as our major national economic problem, producing big and negative effects. The balance of trade deficit supposedly grew from the budget deficit because it produced high interest rates, which in turn led to increased foreign lending to the United States, a squeeze on capital formation, and an overvalued dollar. Only a few in the legislature dissented from this, and they were either left-liberals or a small group of Republican supply-siders centered around Jack Kemp. For the two wings, the deficit should not be reduced at the expense of either essential domestic government or the ongoing revolution in incentives (pick one).

It is striking that the stock and bond markets drew so little mention as important influences on the economy. Budget debates often mention the markets as barometers of business health and confidence, and the stock crash of 1987 did force some hasty "peak bargaining" over deficit reduction between president and

TABLE 2–2   Practical Theories of the Economy in Congress in 1986[1]

Influences on the Economy	House (N = 253)			Senate (N = 67)		
Percentage saying strong influence	Northern Dem.	Southern Dem.	Republican	Northern Dem.	Southern Dem.	Republican
Budget deficits	51	86	65*	65	63	61
Interest rates	48	38	61*	39	38	56
Balance of trade deficits	55	64	26*	57	38	28*
Oil prices	43	36	41	44	25	47
Tax policy	27	24	31	17	25	14
Stock & bond markets	7	—	4	13	—	3
Problem areas of the economy						
Percentage identifying as a problem	Northern Dem.	Southern Dem.	Republican	Northern Dem.	Southern Dem.	Republican
Budget deficits	65	83	81*	78	100	92*
Balance of trade deficits	72	81	47*	78	75	58
Unemployment	47	31	15*	35	38	8*
Inflation	3	2	—	—	—	—
Productivity growth	28	24	29	39	50	19
Interest rates	16	14	15	13	—	11

[1] All figures are percentages of the group listed in each column.
* Differences in percentage among the three groups in this row are significant at the .05 level.

Congress. But it may be that the markets influence voting only when they act in extreme fashion, serving as interpreters of danger signals from the economy. Former House Budget committee chair James Jones suggested as much: "The markets are important to the extent that they illustrate other economic problems or conditions through their own actions. You watch the markets to see how the business community is reading the economy. That can be helpful in sorting out the economy for yourself." Lawmakers' broad receptivity to conventional wisdom grew from the fact that many of them lacked analytical tools for understanding what was happening in the economy and so turned to experts featured in the national media, many of whom were in the financial community. Hence the ascendancy of the political stratum.

Legislators themselves are not independent founts of economic analysis. Representatives and senators readily can provide a brief statement about the present state of the national economy: "it's pretty shaky" or "looks very sound" are typical comments of this sort. Most have not thought the matter through carefully. Some, like one senior House Democrat, admit that such a thumbnail sketch is based on little understanding of economic relationships: "The economy looks good, but I don't know enough about economics to be able to tell you why." Others can go beyond brief evaluations to explain what key relationships are influencing the course of the economy at present. Not surprisingly, they usually are members of the "economic" committees that have jurisdiction over parts of fiscal policy.[23]

Defining practical theories is a dynamic process for members; a steady stream of information is available to them.[24] Sound comprehension does not come easily. A legislator must put in time and effort in order to understand the workings of the economy. The clarity of one's theories derives from three sources: personal motivation, committee experiences, and analytical prowess. One must either find the topic of great policy import, be exposed to it regularly on "economic" committees, or bring conceptual equipment with you to the job that allows you to interpret economic events for yourself.

Annual floor debates over budget resolutions usually include elementary sorts of practical theories. Lawmakers announce them as a means of gaining support for a particular course of action, theory being the handmaiden of ideology and political strategy, as in the following examples. Representative Bill McCollum (R-Fla.), speaking on behalf of the Gramm-Latta amendment to the budget resolution in 1981:

> For years and years, productivity went up in this nation, and when it did, so did our economy despite the fact that we were ravished by excessive spending. . . . we still have to control and get back into our economy the productivity that made this nation great to control inflation. The only way we can do this is by cutting taxes. . . . The president's and the bipartisan proposal of Latta-Gramm is essential to this because it founds itself on the basic assumptions of tax cuts as well as spending cuts. Until we get that under control, until we look at that, we cannot in any way conceivably control inflation.[25]

Senator J. Bennett Johnston (D-La.) speaking in support of his alternative budget resolution in 1983:

> If the economists are correct in what they tell us, and they are vir- tually united in this, deficits of this size will soon abort the recovery and will bring us to economic stagnation with even higher unemploy- ment than we now have and with other difficulties the likes of which we have never seen. I think the arguments have been made, Mr. President. I simply urge my colleagues who think the situation is as bad as we do, to vote with us.[26]

Though understanding of the national economy varies consid- erably on Capitol Hill, legislators have a more uniformly sound grasp of the economic conditions in their districts and home states. The political incentive to obtain this information is direct— lawmakers must have it in order to service their constituencies' needs. Usually legislators can quickly sketch out the economic base of the constituency and what the prospects are for its various elements. One House Republican leader described this facility as "simple bread and butter politics."

District concerns are evident in Table 2–2 as "problem areas" of the economy. Many northern and southern Democrats in 1986 represented areas hard hit by imports, from the Pennsylvania steel country to the textile factories of South Carolina. The relative imbalance of the economic recovery is reflected in the lesser sali- ence of these problem to Republicans, many from suburban and rural districts enjoying the fruits of economic expansion in services and farm production. One reason Democrats came to oppose strongly the Reagan deficit was the perception that it had created economic conditions that hurt their constituents more so than had the deficits under Jimmy Carter.[27]

Though lawmakers have a manifest incentive to oversee economic conditions back home, the intensity of the incentive does vary. Interest in local economies depends upon a legislator's "representative focus," defined by Roger Davidson as "the particular constituency or constituencies that serve as referents for the legislator's behavior."[28] Those viewing their job primarily as representing local home interests find the economy of the constituency to be a central topic in their worklives. Representative George Wortley (R-N.Y.) was an example: "I know my district well because my main job is to promote it." Those more inclined to vent their energies in the formulation and discussion of national policies are aware of conditions in the constituency, but tend to view them as one element in a national set of concerns. Consider this 1986 statement by Republican Robert Walker of Pennsylvania, then a leader of the Conservative Opportunity Society in the House: "The economy in my district is fine. Unemployment is quite low, and they mainly want me to keep up what I've been doing here, which is fighting the welfare state mentality."

Perception of the economy in the constituency can color one's view of the economic state of the nation. Members whose local economies are in trouble tend to find this symptomatic of national economic weaknesses. Representative Charles Stenholm (D-Tex.), for example, saw his district's economy as "awful" and the national economy as "none too good." The reverse is also true. Representative Judd Gregg (R-N.H.) described his district as experiencing a "boom that should continue" and the nation's economy as in "a strong period."

Practical theories usually interact with ideological beliefs when lawmakers confront budget issues. What is the interplay between the two? When a fiscal vote is viewed primarily in constituency terms, ideology is often in the service of local needs. Locally oriented legislators are particularly inclined to operate to "maintain their programs" or "defend the home turf" as they sometimes put it. They see resolution and particularly reconciliation and appropriations votes as opportunities to help the local economy by preserving particular spending programs. By the mid-1980s, relatively few remained uniformly locally-oriented in their approach to budget votes; most at least discussed resolution votes in "big picture" terms, probably because large deficits required a more broad-based conception in order find a solution. Only a small percentage of those I interviewed discussed budget voting solely in local terms.[29] As a House Republican leader put it: "you really have to think nationally if you're going to solve this problem."

When members adopt a more national focus on fiscal votes, the interaction of theory and ideology follows one of two patterns. One's understanding of the economy may constrain pursuit of ideological goals. For example, consider the statement by Representative Don Pease (D-Ohio): "You have to realize that we live in a capitalist society and take your views from there. We get the message of capitalism from all directions, so the question becomes what should not be determined by the market. A lot of alternatives I otherwise might consider when voting on taxing and spending are ruled out by these considerations." One conservative Senate Republican indicated: "The threat of the deficits to the economy is so great that I've had to accept less for defense than I want. A number of us in both chambers have had to do that."

Alternatively, one's ideology may shape the formulation of practical theories. Some lawmakers adopt explanations in accord with their stabilization ideology due to skepticism that any conventional wisdom can get it right. Two differing House views of the impact of the fiscal policy upon the economy illustrate the tendency. Conservative Mark Siljander (R-Mich.), attributed the 1983–84 recovery to "the unleashing of incentives through tax cuts." But liberal Bruce Morrison (D-Conn.) saw it as a "standard Keynesian, consumption-led recovery brought on by deficit stimulus."

Practical theories and economic ideology drive budget resolution votes more so than those on appropriations or reconciliation. Members commonly referred to a resolution as a "big picture" vote where broad questions about the role of government in the economy are addressed. Senator Thad Cochran (R-Miss.) put it this way: "This is the time when we can look at government overall, so it is no wonder that all sorts of issues are raised on the floor—particularly in the Senate, where our debate time is not tightly limited." A budget resolution vote for many members is a "philosophical vote" that expresses spending priorities. Lawmakers termed it "a vote of my basic values," an "overall statement of where the government should be going," or "a reflection of my basic beliefs."

Economic ideology and practical theories do, however, provide an overall substantive mooring for legislators as they confront the thicket of budget issues. Appropriations and reconciliation may address personal program convictions and "constituency maintenance" spending; resolutions may tap beliefs and practical theories about the national economy. A common thread uniting the two dimensions of behavior is the influence of a prior voting record, mentioned by Kingdon as an important constraint upon voting behavior.[30] Representative John Hiler (R-Ind.) asserted that he had "spent six years going back and forth and talking to my constituents. This resolution vote [in 1986] was an expression of my philosophical standing and few back home would be surprised at it." Senator Dennis DeConcini (D-Ariz.) stated: "My pattern on fiscal voting is pretty consistent for a reason. My basic beliefs, which are pretty much reflected in votes like this, have been stable." Legislators of course claim that they rarely compromise their ideological convictions in the face of opposing pressures when voting on a resolution, reconciliation, or appropriations bill. As guides to choice, however, ideology and practical theories are not always very specific; a particular budget vote can invite the play of a large number of political influences.

DIRECT AND INDIRECT POLITICAL INFLUENCES

By now the results of professed influences upon the FY 1987 budget resolution, displayed in Tables 2–3 and 2–4, should come as no surprise.[31] The reason for the predominance of personal convictions on a resolution vote is not obscure—it involved overall budget totals. Claims such as "this is the great issue of our time," "it's a major crisis for our political system," or "we spend all our time on it because it's so important" issue from the lips of just about every legislator about the broader deficit problem. This is the very definition of a high salience issue; members develop strong and consistent views to guide their votes. Kingdon found such issues were usually driven by personal convictions.[32] Frequent vot-

TABLE 2–3   Influences upon the Senate Vote on the FY 1987 Budget Resolution[1]

Percentage saying very influential	Northern Dem.	Southern Dem.	Republican	Pro-GRH	Other
Personal convictions	96	88	85	92	85
Constituents	50	75	50	57	48*
Party leaders	5	13	40*	32	12
GRH act	32	29	46	58	12**
Staff	38	38	24	22	44
Budget comm. chair or ranking member	18	25	39	27	35
Budget comm. members	5	13	7	9	4
Other colleagues	5	—	10	6	8
President	—	—	16**	14	—**
Lobbyists	—	—	—	—	—

*Differences among or between the groups significant at the .05 level.
**Differences among or between the groups significant at the .01 level.
[1]Overall N = 67. The total number of responses to each of the above items did not always equal 67 as some items were not completed by respondents. Significance tests were conducted for the items by party/region and GRH support/opposition.

TABLE 2–4   Influences upon the House Vote on the FY 1987 Budget Resolution[1]

Percentage saying very influential	Northern Dem.	Southern Dem.	Republican	Pro-GRH	Other
Personal convictions	91	85	96	94	91
Constituents	62	51	58	61	56
Party leaders	47	29	36	41	37
GRH act	22	39	57**	59	24**
Staff	23	20	33	28	26
Budget comm. chair or ranking member	33	26	12**	18	27
Budget comm. members	11	15	6**	8	10
Other colleagues	4	3	8	6	5
President	1	5	33**	27	7**
Lobbyists	3	—	2	—	4

**Differences among or between the groups significant at the .01 level.
[1]Overall N = 253. The total number of responses to each of the above items did not always equal 253 as some items were not completed by respondents. Significance tests were conducted for the items by party/region and GRH support/opposition.

ing on such issues over the decade had given the situation an air of familiarity and had required some thinking about the topic. As Representative Charles Stenholm (D-Tex.) stated: "You can't run from this one, you have to think it through." Another reason to "think it through" is to be able to explain your position back home, one of several ways that constituents influence voting.[33]

John Kingdon further discovered that House members were influenced by their constituencies in a variety of ways: the process of recruitment, the need to explain their votes, direct communication, and fear of electoral consequences.[34] The latter three represent direct constituency influence on a vote and probably figure into the substantial importance of the constituency in resolution voting as evident in Tables 2–3 and 2–4 and in personal interviews.[35] Recruitment, however, is a more indirect and probably overall a more important influence; Kingdon termed it a "profound" shaper of legislators' behavior.[36] That power is the linkage of legislator to constituents through shared attitudes rather than conspicuously applied influence. Representative Howard Neilson (R-Utah) summarized it well:

> It is impossible to take this sort of vote to your constituents and get their advice. You get some general guidelines from them, and then you're on your own. You have to rely upon yourself and your staff to make decisions that are ultimately in their interest. With most members, there's no great electoral risk in this, because the attitudes on issues like this that they share with their constituents got them here in the first place.

Recruitment is a shaper of legislative tendencies, not a dictator of specific actions. Robert Bernstein, in his study of the relationship between constituency and legislator, finds that "members don't have to adopt the positions of their constituencies; they, however, often choose to adopt them."[37] It is entirely possible for members to vote their convictions and in so doing bring to bear the influence of their constituents upon their decision. Kingdon found that in the large majority of votes on major issues, lawmakers perceived no conflict between their convictions and the preferences of their constituents.[38] Members reflect this when commenting, as they often do, about the similarity of their views with those of the folks back home. Representative Tim Penny (D-Minn.), for example, claimed: "My views on the budget match up pretty well with the First District voter." His House colleague Duncan Hunter (R-Cal.) stated: "On budget issues my district is conservative and pro-defense and so am I."[39]

Senators made this admission less frequently. Given that many of them regularly face competitive election campaigns and represent large and diverse constituencies, their perceptions of how their views coincide with those back home tend to refer not to the constituency as a whole but more to their "supporting electoral coalition." House members also think in terms of coalitions,[40] but the greater homogeneity of their constituencies often means that the coalition overlaps more with the constituency as a whole than it ever could statewide for Senators. One Senate Democrat indicated that "I am from a heterogeneous state and can't represent everybody on a big issue like this. I have to go with my views, and hopefully enough people will support me to help me win reelection." The looser linkage between constituency and Senator on such a major issue indicates why the Senate is a more hostile electoral environment for incumbents than the House.[41]

Interest groups seem to be influential upon legislators to the extent that they are perceived as part of the constituency, as Kingdon discovered.[42] In Tables 2–3 and 2–4, the influence of interest groups separate from the constituency appears to be nil. A comment from Representative Claudine Schneider (R-R.I.)[43] illustrates why: "I really don't hear that much from them, and it's just as well, because I would pay little attention to them." In certain instances their influence might increase when a member is ideologically motivated to support them. Representative Peter Kostmayer (D-Pa.), for example, vigorously supported foreign aid even though "my constituency doesn't share my strong convictions about it."

The manner of influence by groups in the constituency varied in its directness. A more indirect form arose from an interest's presence in the mind of the legislator as part of the economic base of the district, or among its political elite. As Representative Cooper Evans (R-Iowa) indicated: "I can't think of my district without thinking of farmers." Congressman Joe Kolter (D-Pa.) claimed: "Steel is the lifeblood of my district." Several Representatives mentioned that they had established "constituency networks" of active supporters who regularly reported both their own views and broader constituent sentiments to the congressional office.

Relatively direct influences came from group appeals to the lawmaker in the form of phone calls, letters, and personal meetings, and more frequently occurred over appropriations and reconciliation than resolution votes. The effectiveness of this is doubtlessly variable, though legislators reported that group demands in such situations became much more temperate as deficits persisted. "They used to demand real increases in their programs, then it dropped to raises to keep up with inflation and now they beg for keeping the program at the same level of nominal funding regardless of inflation," according to Representative Doug Bereuter (R-Nebr.).

Lawmakers commonly reported that any interest group contact on budget votes, which was almost always from groups in the constituency, concerned particular aspects of a resolution, appropriations, or reconciliation bill. "That's all I hear about," said Representative Ben Erdreich (D-Ala.). "The iron triangles are alive and well. Bureaucrats in D.C. will contact interest groups back in the state and soon my phone lines are full of demands that I vote against this or that program cut," claimed Senator David Durenberger (R-Minn.). Reconciliation votes—the "real cuts"—are where groups were most likely to be evident to a legislator. Group pressure usually operated at the program level, reinforcing legislators' allocative and distributive views about spending specifics. Groups seldom mentioned stabilization questions. A grand mandate in support of a comprehensive fiscal proposal, like that accompanying the Reagan budget package in 1981, was a rarity. Interests back home usually had narrower sights.

The constituency thus shapes the thinking of legislators on budget issues in a variety of ways. Practical theories about the economy include a careful appreciation of the district economy. Recruitment produces members whose general views about the deficit tend to mirror important convictions of their electoral coalitions back home. Interest groups gain influence through a constituency connection, reinforcing lawmakers' program-level convictions about allocation and distribution issues. The home coalition supplies and tolerates a legislator with particular ideological views. If members indeed vote their own convictions on budget resolutions, it is the constituencies that permit this behavior to occur.

The president's influence over budget votes was directly quite small but indirectly enormous. It was only effective in a direct sense when lawmakers found his proposals salient and popular at home and ideologically not objectionable. The year 1981 most nearly satisfied these conditions.[44] Even in such circumstances, Reagan's influence did not override that of convictions and constituency, but was successful in that it worked through them to the vote. As a Democratic Senator recalled: "In 1981, the constituency pressure was substantial, and none of us were all that confident that we had the answers, so why not give the president a chance?"

After 1981 it was easier for Ronald Reagan and George Bush to exercise an indirect and negative influence. Allen Schick has noted that annual budget proposals from the White House became mere "opening bids" that effectively foreclosed certain budget options by shrewdly structuring the choice situation:

> When the president adorned his budget with unduly favorable economic forecasts, Congress could not effectively riposte with more austere assumptions. Doing so simply raised the deficit and alienated potential supporters. Similarly, when the president endorsed deep domestic cuts, he put Congress in the unenviable position of having to enact the cutbacks, raise the deficit, or take money from other areas. Each of these options was an anathema to a sizeable contingent of Members.[45]

And of course Presidents Reagan and Bush (until 1990) were dead set against taxes.[46] The key asset for both of them in this was their popularity, well known to members of the rival party in Congress. As one senior House Democrat mentioned about Reagan in 1985: "Everyone in the leadership is afraid of crossing the president on taxes. He is the great communicator, and he can kill us on that issue."

This sort of influence did not translate into direct impact upon specific budget votes of members in either party. Tables 2–3 and 2–4 show that lawmakers of both parties overwhelmingly labeled the president an insignificant influence upon their budget resolution vote in 1986.[47] This was because White House fiscal policy proposals, while strategically effective, were received as less than serious approaches to the deficit problem. One Republican member of the House Budget committee by 1986 was complaining: "We just can't take this stuff seriously. They propose huge deficits and tell us to do something about it. Then they get mad at whatever we try to come up with. They just aren't major players anymore."

By sharply limiting congressional budget options via the president's "opening bid," Bush and Reagan forced "peak negotiation" over acceptable fiscal measures. The veto pen was always available at the end of the talks, and Reagan used it with several spending bills in the mid-1980s to prove his seriousness. A Bush veto forced action on long-term deficit reduction in 1990 by causing a weekend government shutdown. Perhaps the president did not fare too well in directly influencing votes on particular bills, but the powers of his office made his overall impact on budget politics impressive.

Like the president, three other sets of actors—personal staff, party leaders, and institutional analysts (the Congressional Budget Office and Office of Management and Budget)—are more significant for indirectly structuring the environment in which budget voting occurred. Neither staff nor party leaders appear as substantial direct influences upon resolution votes in 1986 as evident in Tables 2–3 and 2–4.[48] But both have indirect effects, more detectable in the case of party leadership.

Party leaders performed an important structuring role in budget voting, but one that was political rather than analytical. This was particularly evident in the House, the institutional bastion of opposition to the president in budget politics from 1981 to 1987. Democratic party leaders there played an important consultative role in the formulation of a budget resolution by the Budget committee majority; the party's Majority Leader sits on the Budget committee. From 1981 to 1984, the Leader's role was secondary to the efforts of Budget committee chair James Jones (D-Okla.) at forging a Democratic resolution in committee. From 1985 to 1988, the Majority Leader worked closely in the majority caucus with Jones's successor, William Gray (D-Pa.), and the committee members, to create, in the words of Marty Russo (D-Ill.), then a committee member, "a resolution that commanded support of enough Democrats to ensure passage." One senior Democratic House member described this as an attempt by the leadership to "find out where the people are and get in front of them." As such it served to frame the main alternative for floor consideration, but not as a result of leadership dictation so much as a desire to prevail by reflecting member desires. The composition of the "Democratic package" structured the course of budget politics in the House after 1982.[49] Republican leaders at times, and, after 1982, unsuccessfully, presented an alternative budget resolution, usually sponsored by Delbert Latta (R-Ohio), ranking minority member on the Budget committee. This pattern continued into the Bush presidency under the committee chair Leon Panetta (D-Cal.) and ranking member Bill Frenzel (R-Minn.).

A less formal structuring process occurred in the Senate. Pete Domenici (R-N.Mex.), Budget committee chair from 1981 to 1987, consulted with the leadership as resolutions were composed. The committee product did not always receive the support of the Republican leadership on the floor, often because it drew the disapproval of the president and most Senate Republicans. In 1985 and 1986, Majority Leader Robert Dole involved himself in a renegotiation of the committee resolution in order to gain chamber passage. Again, a structuring role was evident, but one characterized by responsiveness rather than dictation. The Senate Democratic leadership occasionally and with scant success presented alternative resolutions on the floor during the Republican ascendancy. Domenici's Democratic successors, Lawton Chiles (D-Fla.) in 1987 and James Sasser (D-Tenn.) in 1989, also regularly consulted with his party leadership and caucus when composing resolutions.

Reconciliation involved the leadership much less visibly than did resolutions. The process required authorizing committees to report reconciliation language in conformance with the totals of the resolution, an abstruse process of intercommittee and interchamber bargaining that often grew quite protracted.[50] Reconciliation for FY 1986, for example, was not agreed upon until almost five months of the fiscal year had expired. In such negotiations, party leaders were active but much less likely to dominate the process.

Appropriations and tax politics were another matter altogether. The standing committees in each chamber entrusted with these responsibilities became a "new oligarchy" in the House and, to a lesser extent, in the Senate, as their product came to dominate congressional business. Members of these committees reported great satisfaction at being "where the action is" on the legislative agenda. The tax committees, for example, controlled not only the revenue side of the budget but most entitlements as well. Appropriators had their wings clipped by the 1981 reconciliation process but afterward were not the focus of significant reconciliation discipline. Each committee could continue its routines within a broad deficit constraint, but that left ample room for program politics within the limits.[51]

Given these patterns, it is not surprising to find the direct influence of party leaders on the 1986 resolution vote to have been small, though somewhat substantial in the Senate Republican case, where much leadership-directed negotiation was directly instrumental to its passage. In personal interviews, lawmakers overwhelmingly reported that leader positions on budget votes were of negligible importance on their votes on budget issues.[52] One Republican representative summed up their influence: "Party leaders aren't important to my voting, really; they also don't seek me out most times." As Alan Cranston, Senate Democratic Whip indicated: "We really don't have the means to compel members to follow us on budget issues or any other issue for that matter." Leaders usually are not able to administer reliably punishments to recalcitrant backbenchers. As Representative Jim Moody (D-Wis.) put it: "If the leadership is upset with me, there is little they can do. The sorts of things they can do are trivial, once you have the committee assignments you want. Once you have the committees, you can be an independent operator. Phil Gramm was an out-and-out spy but he kept his Energy and Commerce seat."

The fact remains, though, that resolution votes, particularly in the House, usually produced a majority of Democrats opposing a majority of Republicans. Such partisanship resulted from leaders encouraging the formulation of alternatives acceptable to a majority of their followers. A resolution had to be substantively "balanced," an exercise in leadership responsiveness, not dictation. On resolutions, the overall direction had to be acceptable; passage of reconciliation usually was assured by satisfying program preferences of enough members of the majority party on the budget, authorizing, and appropriations committees. Unity on resolution or reconciliation votes rested upon the satisfaction of party members' fiscal preferences, an imperative underscoring the importance of personal convictions in budget voting.

The failure on the House floor in early October 1990 of a deficit reduction package negotiated by the White House and congressional leadership demonstrated these limits on party leaders' power. House Republicans opposed the higher taxes; Democrats the entitlement cuts. On the difficult issues of reducing spending and hiking taxes, leaders had little room for maneuver—they could only lead their parties by following rank-and-file opinion. No deal could be structured without political support, and that support required a close attention to the program preferences of fellow partisans.

Members in interviews and the results of the questionnaire gave little direct importance to staff in influencing the 1986 resolution vote.[53] Personal staff, committee staff, and institutional analysts exercise indirect influence, though, by providing interpretations of the current fiscal situation both to the Budget committees as they compose resolutions and to individual lawmakers as they contemplate their votes. This does not constitute independent clout, however, because staff hardly constitutes the sole source of such insight. Kingdon found that personal staff members had high levels of agreement with a lawmaker's vote but low levels of influence.[54] Personal and committee staffs usually provide politically nuanced recommendations.

The Congressional Budget Office prides itself, however, on its neutral analyses. It served as an important institutional resource in the budget battles of the decade, for it consistently differed in its economic and budget projections from the president's Office of Management and Budget. Budget committees at times resorted to CBO analysis when they found the president's numbers wanting. CBO, then, helped to structure the war of numbers, as did OMB. Their centrality to budget politics became evident to all during the passage of Gramm-Rudman-Hollings in 1985, as will be noted later.

The faithful service to members generated a large reservoir of good will. Members in interviews often lauded the supplementary role of staff and CBO: "I don't know how we would know what is going on around here without our staffs," said Representative George Brown (D-Cal.). Senator Slade Gorton (R-Wash.), a member of the Senate Budget committee from 1981 to 1987, labeled CBO analysis of "very high quality and to be taken seriously." In contrast, lawmakers by the mid-1980s viewed OMB as an explicitly political arm of the president in budget politics whose analysis could not be trusted.[55]

DISSONANCE AND ULTIMATE ENDS

The above survey of legislative political economy raises the question of how its various aspects interact in congressional thinking. Future chapters will note the signal tension lawmakers faced throughout the 1980s: protect your programs but reduce the deficit. The term "but" is instructive here, for most in Congress found the reconciliation of these two imperatives to be quite difficult. Both had direct consequences for the primary legislative goals of good public policy and reelection. Further, how one resolved this tension could have implications for influence within Washington, given the emphasis of the political stratum upon deficit reduction.

Lawmakers find many good reasons to protect their programs. Programs may be essential to the economic base of one's district, or to continued popularity with one's supporting electoral coalition. Many undoubtedly viewed them as "the programs that made America great," in Tip O'Neill's notable 1981 formulation.[56] Ideological attachment may be strong. But consider the pressing need for deficit reduction after 1981. Attentive constituents probably mentioned it to lawmakers, the national media proclaimed it a major national challenge, and most economists thought it was absolutely essential for the economic future of the country. One got the message that persistent deficits are a sign of poor governance; that you were doing your job poorly by continuing to vote for budget bills that perpetuate them. All the while you struggled to preserve your programs. This tension erupted particularly whenever the debt limit arrived on the Senate floor (the House beginning in 1985 minimized the controversy by including debt increase legislation with its budget resolution) and whenever budget resolutions, reconciliation, or continuing resolutions were debated. As Representative Bill Richardson (D-N.Mex.) said: "This has not been a very fun decade in which to be a legislator."

The concept of "cognitive dissonance" from social psychology helps to illuminate how legislators sought to mitigate their unease. Leon Festinger in his classic work on the subject defined cognition as "any knowledge, opinion or belief about the environment, about oneself, or about one's behavior."[57] Dissonance, or "being psychologically uncomfortable," occurs when the obverse of one cognitive element "would follow from the other."[58] Legislators almost unanimously proclaimed their desire for deficit reduction while voting to maintain large deficits—actions were inconsistent with convictions. Further, the existence of major dissonance in this case became customary. For most in Congress, "two or more established beliefs or values" remained inconsistent throughout the decade.[59] In the language of political economy, allocative and distributive program commitments did not mesh with stabilization imperatives.

The magnitude of this dissonance had to be great for most lawmakers, since magnitude is "a function of the importance of the elements" involved in the dissonance.[60] The political stratum and perhaps one's sense of occupational self-worth required major deficit reduction. The goals of good public policy, and possibly intra-Washington influence, figured in that imperative. But the need to protect programs—*also* a matter of good public policy to each lawmaker and pertinent to reelection—likewise seemed essential. Dissonance reduction strategies were in order.

One can reduce dissonance by either changing one's behavior or one's environment. In this situation, behavior would alter more readily than the external pressures for program protection or deficit reduction. One way to alter behavior is to "add new cognitive elements"—that is, bring additional knowledge to bear in order to reduce tension.[61] Members did manage to reduce the causal link between their own behavior and burgeoning deficits through certain rationalizations that employed new cognitive elements.

One approach involved arriving at the conclusion that the sky was not falling. As the decade wore on, this formulation gained additional supporting evidence and use. Deficits were not producing short-term economic calamity; rather the problem seemed long-term and therefore the immediate stakes were smaller. More liberal lawmakers, less ideologically opposed to deficits, gave voice to this rationale. Representative Morris Udall (D-Ariz.) claimed in 1986 that "the resilience of the economy is putting a lot of economic Cassandras to shame." Representative Major Owens (D-N.Y.) voiced skepticism of "all this deficit mania. You'd think it was the only problem we had. Poverty and oppression are everywhere around us, yet we focus on a problem that may or may not be serious." A few supply-side Republicans, most notably Jack Kemp, shared the skepticism. But many legislators not of the left or visionary right could not accept the argument. Senator Max Baucus (D-Mont.) argued that "the problem is with us, and the economic consequences may be severe. We are playing Russian roulette with the economy." Representative Harris Fawell (R-Ill.) remarked that "I don't want to wait to see what happens. I think the consequences will be so terrible. We have to act now." Representative Leon Panetta (D-Cal.), perhaps in the center of Democratic party opinion, claimed that "deficits are at the root of a number of economic problems and we have to act now." The persuasiveness of the political stratum made this rationalization acceptable to only a relative few.

The more common set of reasons employed to reduce dissonance can be summarized under the phrase "it's not my fault." Yes, the deficit was bad, its perpetuation worse. Yes, worthy programs must be preserved. But, thought the intrepid legislator, I have a deficit reduction plan in mind, and if others do not agree, is it my fault? Conclusion: common sense had deserted my political opponents, hence deficits. Representative Frank Guarini (D-N.J.) held that "as soon as the administration decides to be realistic, the problem can be solved." Robert Dornan, the fiery Republican House conservative from California, asserted that "the political problem of deficits lies in the addiction of the Democratic party to domestic spending. Only by attacking this can we get deficits under control." Clearly, this was an argument that coordinated nicely with the ubiquitous partisan instincts of legislators.

One could further convince oneself that deficits were the fault of others by recalling the legitimate program claims of constituents. Liberal Representative Carl Perkins (D-Ky.) held that "the budget will not be balanced on the backs of my people, if I can at all avoid it. They have suffered from the cuts of the early 1980s and are hurting." Antitax zealot William Dannemeyer (R-Cal.) undoubtedly reflected the feelings of many Republican colleagues when he stated that "taxes are too high as is. The people in my district work hard and pay too much to government already. The last thing they and I want are higher taxes." When you are fighting the good fight for the people who elected you, it is easier to blame others and feel not at all at fault for your defensive maneuvers.

The 1980s in Congress give testament to Festinger's assertion that "the resistance to change of the cognitive element is identical with the resistance to change of the behavior reflected by that element."[62] As legislators repeated the rationalizations year after year, a die was cast allowing members to reduce dissonance to a personally acceptable level. The cumulative result bears resemblance to the example of the Ifaluk, a preliterate society. The Ifaluk believed people were good, but also found that their children went through a phase of destructive behavior, in contradiction to the first belief. The solution? Addition of a third belief that malevolent ghosts possessed the children when they acted in this fashion.[63] The most common thought sequence in Congress was similar, involving the following elements: (1) deficits are bad and should be addressed, but (2) I vote for large deficits every year, therefore (3) devils (political opponents) are the reason I am forced to do this despite pure intentions on my part.[64] The logical sequence was widely employed and effective because it was rooted firmly in truth—the differing preferences over the content of deficit reduction did forestall it. And it gave legislators a justification that would allow them to look at themselves in the mirror without blinking on most mornings.

Dissonance reduction strategies explain the spectacular failure of the political stratum throughout the decade to induce a deficit reduction panic. Not that they did not try. As White and Wildavsky state: "We have seen commentators galore, the mass media and academics, holding politicians accountable; the newsweeklies running cover articles on the deficit monster searching for ill effects and, as they stubbornly refused to appear, concluding that retribution was inevitable."[65] When the sky did not fall, lawmakers had every incentive to look for arguments why deficits did not matter as much as had been thought. Constituents seemed to want deficit reduction but did care how it was accomplished; not all means were acceptable.[66] Legislators then supplied the arguments against various means.

It is not surprising that coping strategies became necessary for lawmakers, given the massive scale of the dissonance they confronted.[67] For most of them, conflict registered in important aspects of personal political economy and in direct relationship to member goals. Ideologically, allocative and distributive program beliefs clashed with the stabilization imperative of lower deficits. Thus the very definition of good policy was unsettled. Would the effects be dramatic in the short-term or long-term, or never? No one could be sure, further complicating the question of good policy. The political imperative of constituency protection also collided with notions of the national good, potentially threatening reelection. And "doing the right thing" for the nation might help one's stature in Washington at the expense of votes back home— reelection versus intra-Washington influence.

Lawmakers could find avenues for rationalization even in the wake of the controversial deficit reduction of 1990. Pressure for a serious long-term deal came from the White House and party leadership. For many legislators, the choice between deficit reduction and constituency protection was complicated by Bush's firm demand that action be taken before Congress could adjourn for the election campaign. Almost half the members of each chamber responded the usual way—by voting no on the plans and blaming others or discounting the importance of the deficits. But just enough lawmakers voted for the plan to secure its passage. Why would they do so? The electoral costs of failure might be high, for one, and the president remained a useful scapegoat. Once the bill passed, legislators who voted yes could accuse the president of holding government hostage in order to further his agenda, and argue that they had fought to protect constituents to the maximum extent possible. Even those who supported the package could argue it was not their fault.

Chapter 5 notes how Gramm-Rudman-Hollings served as a concession by legislators to their own sense of responsibility and to the demands of the political stratum when the deficit was peaking in 1985. But GRH was evaded repeatedly because time did dissipate these inner conflicts for legislators. The sky did not fall (though, as we will see, it looked shaky in October 1987), and other players in Washington deserved blame and continued to help diminish personal tension and guilt. When pressure finally arose for long-term deficit reduction in 1990, it came from the White House and party leadership, and convincing the members of Congress to go along was a very hard sell. The following chapters chart the rise of personal dissonance as evident in the institutional behavior of Congress during the decade. I begin with examination of events leading to a period of uncharacteristically low dissonance over fiscal matters for many legislators—the Reagan revolution of 1981.

CHAPTER 3

Stabilization Fashions of 1979–1981

Much has been written describing the congressional budget maelstrom of 1979 and 1980 and the "intellectual revolution" of supply-side economics in 1981, as if the national legislature under extraordinary circumstances diverged from its usual ways of transacting fiscal business. Some conditions of that period were unusual, but the underlying fiscal judgments of legislators displayed a certain resilience during the time.

The fiscal transformation of 1979–81 grew from legislators' desperate need for successful stabilization tactics that would do no great violence to their programmatic goals. Such goals remained constant, but individual legislators found satisfying them quite difficult in an environment of high inflation and erratic economic growth. For many, the period involved a search for political-economic consistency to lessen dissonance and its attendant stresses.[1] Clearly, an opening existed for stabilization tactics that comported with political needs. Hence the advent of a new theoretical wrinkle in the midst of uncertainty: supply-side economics.

Democrats could not discover such a philosopher's stone. Divided as they were between a vaguely Keynesian mainstream and more conservative southern faction, intraparty consensus on a stabilization course was not forthcoming. Liberal Keynesians continued to decry rising unemployment and urge spending to combat it in the midst of record peacetime inflation. But the creed of deficit spending for social programs was challenged by a growing public and Washington consensus that deficits were the root cause of inflation and that the Soviet invasion of Afghanistan required a substantial increase in defense spending. Conservative southern Democrats supported the new prodefense and antidomestic spending impetus. An embattled group of "fiscal centrists" in the party, notably including the Budget committee chairs of the late 1970s,

Senator Edmund Muskie (D-Me.) and Representative Robert Giamo (D-Conn.), sought to avoid too much or too little fiscal "stimulus" in response to unacceptable levels of unemployment and inflation.

Republican legislators groped for an alternative perspective in the late 1970s. Traditional calls for fiscal rectitude, popular with many staunchly Republican constituencies, ran the risk of stifling growth in an already slumping economy. That was tactically unacceptable. A few enterprising economists and legislators began to purvey a new stabilization theory that promised to avoid such political difficulties. The actual definition of "supply-side" economics never crystalized in common form in Washington. Many Republicans and conservative Democrats remained uncertain and skeptical of its tenets, even as they endorsed a budget course predicated upon them. Political forces made the difference; the help of a popular new president, supply-side argument became the reigning theme in the 1981 Reagan budget revolution.

This chapter examines how new theoretical strategies for economic stabilization found their way into the political economy of congressional budgeting from 1979 to 1981. Entrenched allocation and distribution attitudes, reinforced by constituency linkages, did not provide a ready guide for understanding simultaneous high inflation and unemployment. A change in macroeconomic theories might for the moment point to a tactical way out of the problems—or so some legislators thought. That a popular president with a constituency-based mandate might call for this made the choice plain enough to a majority of the members of both chambers.

THE LATE 1970S

First, some economic context is in order. Jonathan Rauch has described the late 1970s as a time when government's fiscal latitude inexorably began to shrink.[2] The reasons for this were three. First, slowing economic growth caused government to increase steadily its percentage of GNP as it increased spending. Second, inflation produced income tax "bracket creep," which increased individuals' proportional tax burden, raised public ire, and helped to touch off the tax revolt of 1978. Third, the perceived need to increase the

amount of defense expenditures, by three percent annually according to President Carter's 1979 and 1980 budget proposals, put
increased pressure on domestic spending.

Serious deficit problems for the early 1980s were on their way
well before the decisions of 1981. Virtually the entire increase in
spending from 1979 to 1985 came from four areas: Social Security
and Medicare (both entitlements, the former political sacrosanct
and the latter an inviting target), defense (enjoying adequate political support until mid-decade), and interest payments (unavoidable). The defense buildup began in 1979, with most of the Reagan
increases not showing up in spending until 1983. Social Security
grew from 4.3 to 5.2 percent of GNP from 1979 to 1983, due to a
shrinking GNP during the 1981–82 recession and the preceding
stagflation. All this suggests that "only part of the trouble was
avoidable," and that "given the behavior of the economy" during
this time, "any Congress would have faced a serious deficit problem by 1983."[3]

This combination of circumstances by the late 1970s placed
the Democratic majorities in the House and Senate in difficult
fiscal situations, at times leading to the defeat of leadership-
endorsed budget resolutions.[4] Democratic legislators simply differed substantially on how to address the unpleasant fiscal real-
ities. Conservatives urged more for defense and less for domestic
spending, liberals the opposite. All this made life difficult for the
party's budget captains.

In the era of the shrinking margin, intellectually venturesome
Republicans like Representative Jack Kemp (R-N.Y.) found new
political opportunities. They were in tune with the popular belief
in increased defense spending, and echoed public resentments in
their denunciations of the confiscatory effects of bracket creep.
And their supply-side approach promised a thorough solution to
the fundamental problem of the time: economic stabilization.

It was clear to most legislators that a crisis of economic management was underway; beyond that obvious point, confusion re-
igned. A foggy legislative understanding of the concepts of economic stabilization made possible the fragmentation of the
Democratic response to the crisis and the advent of supply-side
economics in Republican ranks. Democrats adopted explanations
of the problem consistent with their economic ideologies, produc-

ing division in their ranks. A growing number of Republicans found supply-side theory ideologically congenial and comprehensible in simple microeconomic terms. When confused, educated laypersons rely on ideology and adopt a perspective they can understand.

The budget debates of the late 1970s are showcases of this behavior. In 1977 and 1978, Giamo and Muskie would present a "cautiously stimulative" budget and defend it in Keynesian terms. A variety of amendments would ensue, aimed at altering the resolution's allocative, distributive, or stabilization framework. Liberal Democrats urged more domestic spending; Republicans wanted domestic rollbacks, defense increases, and tax cuts. The discussion was couched in terms of current economic conditions, the reasons for them, and the economy's short- and medium-term prospects. Muskie prevailed more consistently than Giamo, thanks to the bipartisan cooperation of the ranking Republican of the Senate committee, Henry Bellmon.[5]

By 1979 and 1980, a more vexing economic environment created prodigious stabilization difficulties. In the House, Democratic divisions intensified, producing defeat for the first budget resolution in 1979 and for a resolution conference report in 1980. Liberal Democrats in particular refused to countenance budget austerity requiring what were to them unwarranted cuts in domestic programs and increases in defense spending. In the Senate, the bipartisan Budget committee product continued to enjoy success thanks in large part to Bellmon's efforts, even in 1980 when the loquacious Ernest Hollings (D-S.Car.) replaced Muskie as chair of the committee.

BUDGET DISCUSSION IN THE LATE 1970S

Though the state of the economy and the arguments accounting for it varied considerably from 1977 to 1980, the root ideological perspectives of the legislators debating and voting on budget resolutions altered relatively little during this time. Allocation and distribution priorities remained largely fixed; new stabilization wrinkles entered the debate gradually. Supply-side economics did not burst upon the scene in 1981, but rather first appeared in budget debates in 1977 and recurred frequently until its triumph in the budget and tax votes of 1981. From 1977 to 1980, Republicans proposed various supply-side fiscal packages and Democrats reacted with increasing defensiveness as they struggled to control policy. By 1980, Republicans extolled a variety of what they termed supply-side approaches that promised to solve both immediate and longer-term economic problems, though GOP consensus on a specific tax and budget strategy bearing that label was far from established. "Supply-side" meant many things to many people.

All this occurred in an economic climate hardly noted for its quiet and calm. Inflation had reached double-digit levels in 1979 and 1980, and the GNP plunged an alarming 9.9 percent in the second quarter of 1980. The crisis pitted the need for effective stabilization strategies and tactics against the allocation and distribution preferences of legislators—a troubling dissonance of goals. Conflict was most evident in Democratic ranks, as the following excerpts from debates in 1979 and 1980 demonstrate. Republicans were increasingly coalescing around an alternative that promised escape from such vexations. Allocation, distribution, and stabilization preferences could be satisfied through budget cuts and, more importantly, tax cuts. Personal marginal rate cuts? Accelerated depreciation schedules? Lower capital gains taxes? Indexing tax rates? Each found some Republican support.

FISCAL DEBATE IN 1979–80

The major substantive transformation during this time occurred in stabilization policy, a shift not evident in the views of all members. More intensely committed liberals and conservatives evidenced no great change in their views of fiscal management. Rather, they continued to prescribe macroeconomic policy consistent with their long-held beliefs about the national government's proper size and efforts at redistribution. Liberal Representative Ted Weiss (D-N.Y.) in 1979: "Inflation can only be halted through the enactment of standby controls on wages, prices, and profits, and by providing full employment. Swelling the ranks of the jobless has not worked before, and it certainly will not work now."[6] Conservative Senator Malcolm Wallop (R-Wyo.) in 1980: "Most Americans expect that when they demand that Congress balance the budget, and it is evident they are making such demands, Congress should actually be decreasing spending. . . . Instead we have a budget that only slows the increase in spending and seeks balance by increasing taxes."[7]

Supply-side arguments adopted by congressional conservatives involved a shift in stabilization tactics, not basic strategic convictions. Tax cuts had long been a staple of GOP strategy, if accompanied by spending reductions. But the specific tactics advocated by lawmakers varied considerably in their substance. House Republicans in 1979 presented no less than four alternative budget resolutions, and one would not have cut taxes significantly.[8] Two conservative alternative budget resolutions presented on the Senate floor in 1980 sought to reduce taxes and spending, but neither called for an across-the-board cut in personal income tax rates that was to be the hallmark of the Reagan tax program.[9] Government should tax and spend less—Republican fiscal strategy by 1980 was not more precise in its specification of policy than that. Hence the variety of tactical variations.

It was the ideologically more flexible members of Congress— those whose ideological convictions were tempered by economic and consequent political discomfort—who directed the tactical shift to less expansive fiscal policy after 1978. Business and constituent concerns over rising inflation provided the impetus. The 1977 preoccupation of congressional Democrats with the degree and type of Keynesian fiscal stimulus became by 1979 and 1980 a growing resolve to moderate inflation through spending restraint. Budget chair Ernest Hollings proclaimed on the Senate floor in 1980: "Two years ago, the Senate Budget committee identified inflation as our nation's most serious domestic concern. The Senate agreed. . . . A balanced federal budget is a necessary beginning in a national battle against inflation."[10] Spending was to be redirected from discretionary domestic programs toward defense at the behest of President Carter. In tandem with this approach, the Federal Reserve Board in 1979 had abandoned stable interest rates as a goal and sought to directly control the supply of money in order to combat inflation. By 1980 a policy of cautious fiscal austerity was in place.

Congress took unprecedented steps in making the policy stick. An obscure part of the budget law known as "reconciliation" was invoked in a new way to force cuts in domestic program authorization levels so they would conform to the limits set in the first budget resolution for FY 1981.[11] The Budget act allowed reconciliation with the binding second resolution, to be passed in September, just before the advent of the new fiscal year. Section 301, however, further permitted any procedure "considered to be appropriate to carry out the purpose of this act." So why not discipline the process at the front end by adding it to the previously nonbinding "advisory" first resolution in the spring? A "serious signal" of fiscal restraint could result. House authorizing committee chairs resisted but were overruled on the House floor in their attempt to strip reconciliation language from the first resolution. This was a foretaste of the battles between budget parts and the whole that would erupt throughout the 1980s when efforts to restrain the deficit conflicted with entrenched allocation and distribution preferences of legislative committees. The final reconciliation bill required $8.2 billion in authorization level reductions; a small victory for the perspective of the whole.

The success was quite finite because despite the avowed resolve of Congress to balance the budget in 1980, the economy did not cooperate. The deficit for FY 1981 finally totaled $78.9 billion, thanks to low growth, over seven percent unemployment, and high inflation. Little in fiscal policy by 1980 promised stimulus to overcome these problems. Polls showed the public in favor of budget balance and increased funds for defense and increasingly supportive of tax reductions and cuts in overall levels of spending.[12] Many long-time Republican views suddenly seemed salable as fiscal tactics: less overall allocation, budget balance, more for defense and tax relief. Could they cohere in a politically palatable economic plan? That task fell to Ronald Reagan's OMB director-designate, David Stockman, over three short months: November, December, and January of 1981.

UNDERSTANDING 1981

The extraordinary events of 1981—the adoption of a reconciliation measure of unprecedented size ($35 billion) and of an economic policy of unprecedented tax cuts—have been chronicled abundantly.[13] A focus on the political economy of legislators leads first to the concepts of supply-side economics, and the differing positions found among those espousing the term. In a general sense, "supply-side" thinking enframed the 1981 congressional budget debate, but the phrase served to connote a passing tactical fashion, not a lasting fiscal orthodoxy. Supply-side could be defined and packaged in any number of ways, and made politically palatable to many elected politicians and constituents. Political influences carried the new fashion to success—Congress approved tax and spending reductions structured in the doctrine's name— because it was pressed by a popular president who was perceived to have strong support back home.[14]

Once the first budget resolution for FY 1982 established the general direction of fiscal policy, more traditional programmatic politics became manifest during consideration of the reconciliation and tax bills. It was here that legislators fought for specific types of allocation and distribution, in the time-tested manner of the pork barrel.[15] It would be wrong, however, to characterize these conflicts as only involving district pork. The politics of reconciliation and tax legislation often involved members simultaneously defending their ideological convictions and protecting parts of the supporting electoral coalition back home.[16] But the battle was on new ground; tax reductions were handed out liberally and spending options constricted for the foreseeable future, all as a result of an administration program devised through a ritual of political compromise over disparate economic theories. Its creator, David Stockman, had seen such accommodations before, having participated in the fiscal wars from 1977 to 1980 as a Representative from Michigan.

SUPPLY-SIDE: STABILIZATION THEORY AS TACTICAL FASHION

Stockman, like the vast majority of legislators, was not an economist. Yet he was taken by supply-side theory and tried to clarify it beyond the broad and woolly formulations resonating through legislative halls in 1979 and 1980. Some of its original proponents had attempted a more precise formulation grounded in neoclassical economics, and Stockman had given them his ear. Arthur Laffer, of curve fame, stated in 1980: "Supply-side economics is nothing more than classical economics in modern dress. It basically looks to incentive."[17] Norman Ture, who served as assistant treasury secretary for tax policy from 1981 to 1982, recalled that in the late 1960s he "turned to neoclassical price theory to find explanations of why different tax changes affect the economy in ways they do. Supply-side economics really is just the application of price theory to the analysis of governmental fiscal actions."[18]

Laffer and Ture directed attention to the microeconomic effects of federal policy, particularly tax policy. Prices affect human behavior at the margin, and in microeconomic analysis it is marginal cost that explains whether people will purchase goods, exert labor, or risk investment. Thus the primary variable influencing the growth of the economy is the rate of taxation at the margin. If you lower marginal tax rates, economic growth will increase, producing at least a partial offset of new revenues to compensate for those lost through the original tax cut.[19] Budget policy, in sharp contrast to Keynesian prescriptions, has little effect upon the macroeconomy. Paul Craig Roberts, assistant treasury secretary for economic policy from 1981 to 1982, argued that "in this new policy the deficit is an almost irrelevant side effect of restructuring the tax code. . . . In our approach deficits are removed from being an instrument of policy."[20] This original, "pure" view of supply-side emphasized personal tax cuts. The Kemp-Roth tax cut bill, introduced in 1978 by Representative Jack Kemp (R-N.Y.) and Senator William Roth (R-Del.) sought sharp (30%) reductions in marginal income tax rates on the basis of this rationale.

By 1980, however, a number of politicians and lobbyists were pressing less for individual tax cuts and more for a reduction of the tax and regulatory burden upon business as a means to economic growth. The goal in this was to facilitate more investment, both by individuals and business. Business lobbyists such as Charls Walker, a Treasury official under President Nixon, more orthodox conservatives such as Representatives James Jones (D-Okla.) and Barber Conable (R-N.Y.), ranking Republican on the Ways and Means committee, and the outgoing Carter administration all favored this approach.[21] Jones claimed that "concern with the amount of business investment is the true supply-side approach. That is how you most effectively stimulate production. The ACRS (Accelerated Cost Recovery System, which would accelerate depreciation write-offs for purchases of plant, equipment, and vehicles) is a good example of a supply-side taxation approach. That is what the country needed in 1981." For Jones, cutting personal tax rates was "a sort of Keynesian approach, because people will consume with the money they receive from the cut."

Certain "purist" supply-siders disputed the need for reforms such as ACRS. Jude Wanniski, an early supply-side advocate, termed "changes in the amount of money in corporate coffers for use in buying goods and services and investing in plant and equipment . . . central to demand-side analysis."[22] David Stockman labeled ACRS (or 10–5–3, so entitled for the time allowable for various write-offs) not a "supply-side concept."[23] Politics demanded a more inclusive definition, though. By 1981, versions of both the Kemp-Roth and 10–5–3 proposals were included in the administration's tax reform program. Stockman viewed it as "the price we had to pay for a semblance of GOP unity on tax policy."[24]

Supply-side theorists, though few in number, had gained an appreciative audience in some Republican circles. Though Jack Kemp and Stockman seemed to worship at the shrine in 1980, more orthodox fiscal conservatives such as Robert Dole (R-Kan.), chair of the Senate Finance committee and Conable of the House Ways and Means committee had serious doubts about the effect of tax cuts upon the deficit. Many legislators did not clearly understand the formulation or see an inconsistency in embracing both 10–5–3 and Kemp-Roth. By 1980 the term supply-side was in vogue and subject to indiscriminate usage. Republicans in that year endorsed 10–5–3 and Kemp-Roth as a "supply-side" package. David Stockman recalled a meeting of the House Republican Policy committee in the spring where the approach was approved: "The time had come to settle upon a Republican alternative to the Carter budget. It was incredibly noisy and contentious. . . . Politicians, like baby goslings, go through an 'imprinting' in the infancy of every major new issue. They learn where they stand and what side they're on. . . . 'It might be possible to cut taxes, raise defense, and balance the budget,' they began to think."[25]

Political circumstance dictated the suspension of ideological confusion and the donning of a new fashion. The switch grew from the urgent need for consensus on politically salable stabilization tactics and the pleasant conformity of supply-side tactics with long-standing GOP views on the size of government. Republicans could demand budget and tax cuts, and find broad popular receptivity to claims of their tonic effects—no dissonance of political and ideological goals in that!

What moved GOP thinking in this vague supply-side direction was the economic program proposed by Ronald Reagan.[26] The core assumptions of the program were ones long espoused by Reagan: that (1) economic growth would increase if incentives were improved through changes in taxing, regulation, and spending, and (2) government wastes resources and must be placed on a strict allowance. This drive to limit government size lay at the core of Reagan's "moral economy" or economic ideology. Less allocation above all.[27] During the campaign season, Reagan's program entailed four goals: (1) a balanced budget by 1983, (2) Kemp-Roth and 10–5–3 tax cuts, (3) an anti-inflationary monetary policy, and (4) regulatory reform.[28] Reagan approved the broad outlines of this package, but Stockman had to arrange the policy specifics for the budget and articulate the stabilization strategy underlying the plan.

THE REAGAN PLAN

The administration proposed actions consistent with long-held allocation and distributive preferences of Republicans: a large increase in defense spending, $38 billion in reductions in domestic spending, a big tax cut. The central problem of plausibility involved the costs of the spending and tax cut sides of the plan, and supply-side theory was to be the bailing wire holding the dollar estimates of the two together, making the fiscal tactics defensible. David Stockman loosely constructed the theory from a variety of assumptions and compromises. His effort vividly demonstrated the inexperience of legislators with fiscal theory. It further revealed how political considerations can drive stabilization thinking, as they shaped his arbitrarily selective raiding of theoretical propositions.

Stockman won the OMB job in large part because of a memo on economic policy written for Reagan during the transition period. Entitled "Avoiding a GOP Economic Dunkirk," it detailed the economic ideology and practical theory that would guide the administration and many of its congressional supporters through the 1981 budget season. "In all President Reagan will inherit thoroughly disordered credit and capital markets, punishingly high interest rates, and a hair-trigger market psychology poised to respond strongly to early economic policy signals in either favorable or unfavorable ways."[29] The reason for this volatility was the persistence of "long-term inflation pessimism" caused by "the explosive growth of out-year federal liabilities, spending authority, and credit absorption."[30] Excessive federal allocation had produced the economic problems and threatened to exacerbate them; a common Republican theme. But the potential for dramatic, constructive change did exist.

Given this explanation, the strategic task was one of "elimination of deficits and excessive rates of spending growth."[31] "This means that the policy initiatives designed to spur output growth and to lower inflation expectations and interest rates must carry a large share of the fiscal stabilization burden."[32] A variety of tax changes—a sort of kitchen-sink supply-side approach—would spur growth: Kemp-Roth, lowering the top personal marginal rate from 70 to 50 percent, further reductions in capital gains taxes, and 10–5–3 depreciation changes.[33] By including so many types of cuts, supply-side could be many things to many people and gain political support, a sort of politics of tactical inclusion. Domestic spending would have to be reduced thirty to fifty billion in FY 1982 in order to make room for the "necessary" increase in defense spending in response to growing security threats from the Soviets and Mideast. The administration also was to defend Federal Reserve Board efforts to reduce money supply growth, a relatively monetarist position that would soon land Stockman in hot water with Ture, Roberts, Wanniski, and Laffer, but one widely accepted by more orthodox conservative economists such as Alan Greenspan and Herbert Stein.

Victories in several discrete battles in Congress would be necessary to implement the tactics. First, passage of a budget resolution; second, adoption of a reconciliation bill detailing the cuts; and third, approval of the administration's tax initiative. The task might have been insuperable but for the unprecedented implementation the year before of reconciliation with the first budget resolution. Reconciliation instructions were to be included with the first resolution in 1981, mandating $38 billion in cuts of the Carter administration's "current services" base.[34] The product of Stockman's frenzied three months of activity, these cuts included changes in the authorization levels of numerous domestic programs.[35] Many long-standing allocation preferences of conservative Republicans made the list. Among the proposals were reductions in eligibility for food stamps, AFDC, elimination of supplemental unemployment benefits, increases in deductible payments for Medicare, reductions in federal contributions for Medicaid, elimination of Social Security payments for college students, and elimination of minimum Social Security benefits.

In addition to reconciliation instructions, the resolution would have to provide a revenue number adequate to accommodate the administration's tax cut plans and a defense number allowing a $27 billion increase in outlays over FY 1981. This meant tolerating a substantial deficit in FY 1982—hardly Republican boilerplate, but these were trying times. The administration's budget proposals provided for $695.3 billion in outlays, $650.3 billion in revenues, a tax cut of $51.3 billion, and a $45 billion deficit. The defense spending increases would have major budgetary impact in the out-years. Pentagon outlays were scheduled to increase under the administration plan from $161 billion in FY 1981 to $253 billion in 1984.

Despite such complications, Stockman's proposal also provided for a balanced budget by 1984. This calculational feat became known as the adoption of "rosy scenario," a series of economic assumptions providing for high growth and moderate disinflation in the early 1980s. They resulted from an awkward process of compromise between supply-side and more traditionally conservative economic advisors of the president.[36] The major excess was in predicting that economic growth would proceed at a 5.2 percent annual rate in the latter half of 1981 and 1982. Combined with a 7.2 percent inflation rate prediction for 1982, this produced a revenue surge for the Treasury that would mitigate the budgetary effect of the tax cut plans.[37] The administration's "practical theory" assumed these effects would result from the transformation of expectations its policy changes would promote. Supposedly, the new fiscal policy would connote to the private sector a lasting change in governmental perspective and behavior. This in turn would produce a rapid and favorable adjustment of markets similar to that which the fabled rational maximizer of economics might undertake. This strategic premise derived from Stockman's simplistic understanding of the theory of "rational expectations," and underlay administration economic projections.[38] The economic assumptions, and the gaggle of theories behind them, became a major point of contention during the 1981 budget season in Congress.

A DAY AT THE RACES

A glance at the lengthy race-card for 1981 indicates why the budget debate itself did not capture the variety and intensity of the forces producing policy change in Congress. This became the year of economic theory on the House and Senate floors because the scale of the changes debated dwarfed any attempt to examine their particulars in detail.[39] Though congressional discussion dwelled on the conceptual foundations of the Reagan program, much of the politics of 1981 occurred outside the chambers and concerned program specifics. Constituents, party leaders, and above all the president joined the fray. Reagan's adroit politicking served to keep the process moving in his direction to an extraordinary degree.

Congress had to a great extent been remade in a conservative image. Republicans enjoyed a 53–47 advantage in the Senate, and, along with southern Democrats, could constitute a conservative policy majority in the House. New budget captains had emerged. Pete Domenici (R-N. Mex.), chair of the Senate Budget committee, hoped to assist the administration. Howard Baker (R-Tenn.), the new Majority Leader, was similarly inclined. James Jones (D-Okla.), a moderate conservative, faced a much more ticklish situation as new chair of the House committee. Elected by one vote over liberal David Obey of Wisconsin by the House Democratic caucus, Jones confronted the problem of building support for an alternative to the administration's policies among a divided and dispirited group of Democrats who had seen their majority reduced by thirty-four seats, from 277 to 243.

A successful approach would have to confront the differing politics of budget resolutions and reconciliation. Recall that resolutions are "philosophical votes" and "general statements of direction" that, even with reconciliation instructions, do not legally mandate specific program changes. It is through the reconciliation process, as various authorizing committees develop proposals for meeting the targets found in the "functional categories" for spending in a resolution, that specific expenditure levels are altered.[40] Sweeping alterations of spending would be possible if the votes were there for an administration reconciliation plan. As John Gilmour notes, "insofar as majorities are able to agree on policy, the budget process with reconciliation allows them to get their way."[41] The stakes and political actors were quite distinct between the resolution and reconciliation arenas. Programs are the currency of particular benefits for legislators, constituents, and interest groups—and are "on the block" in reconciliation bills.

In contrast, the general nature of resolution votes made the 1981 Reagan-supported resolutions an "easy vote" for members ideologically sympathetic to the administration and facing considerable pressure from constituents to support its proposals. No actual cuts were mandated by the resolutions, though accompanying reconciliation instructions did establish binding savings targets by function. Calculating attainment of these targets depended upon the spending and savings assumptions the calculators employed; this left much room for creativity. As House Minority Leader Robert Michel (R-Ill.) stated to some of his nervous colleagues at the time: "When are you guys going to realize that this is only a budget resolution? It doesn't cut anything. It's all assumptions."[42]

The fight over the resolution produced the first major administration victory in pitched battle. Though the Senate generally followed the White House lead, the House remained a potential bastion of partisan opposition to the administration. The Democratic leadership sharply opposed the program priorities of the administration, but Democratic ranks were divided. James Jones recalled: "My problem was attempting to satisfy the leadership and caucus on one side and more conservative Democrats on the other. The leadership wanted a successful Democratic alternative to the president. Politically, it became unobtainable in our ranks."

Budget committee Democrats agreed on a resolution providing smaller spending cuts and a one-year tax cut to be more targeted at business than individuals, and more "realistic" economic assumptions than those of the administration. No "radical" cuts like those the administration had proposed.

The hope was that this would keep the Boll Weevils, fiscally conservative southern Democrats, on board by highlighting the key difference between them and Reagan—namely, allocation in the broad sense: "The ultimate stake of the battle, the point where conservative Democrats and moderates most differed from Reagan, was the role of government."[43] It did not work. The administration countered with a floor amendment coauthored by rogue Democrat Phil Gramm (Tex.) and Delbert Latta (R-Ohio), henceforth known as "Gramm-Latta I." After narrowly defeating a rule to prevent the administration-backed package from being considered as a whole, in order to destroy it by defeating some of its parts, the House endorsed Gramm-Latta I by 253–176. Crucial support came from the Boll Weevils.

Once the two chambers settled their few differences over the first resolution, fiscal politics shifted from discussion of the big picture to battles over the preservation, reduction, or elimination of numerous domestic spending programs and the awarding of tax reductions. The deals necessary to secure passage of reconciliation and tax cuts were to undermine the successful implementation of the administration's fiscal tactics. The administration had employed a flawed theory of congressional behavior, as David Stockman later admitted.[44] Though legislators had approved a change in fiscal direction premised upon sweeping nondefense budgetary constraint and specific tax reductions, they did not implement the administration's grand design as planned. Partisanship and competitive bidding for votes cost much in lost expenditure savings and tax revenues. Entrenched program preferences had to be satisfied.

The White House first confronted this problem in the battle over the specific cuts provided the reconciliation bill. The year began promisingly enough for the administration when the Senate adopted reconciliation instructions prior to a budget resolution and eventually produced a reconciliation bill with many of the savings proposed by Stockman. Three factors discouraged the administration's hopes for reconciliation in the House: (1) the partisan makeup made victory questionable and would require specific bargains to attract Boll Weevil votes; (2) the Democratic leadership had been stung by the resolution defeat and was anxious to prevail on reconciliation; and (3) the reconciliation bill would be composed by authorizing committees whose chairpersons were motivated to undermine the limits included in its instructions. Stockman's insistence that the committees had not produced the necessary savings led to the hasty composition of Gramm-Latta II, the administration's alternative reconciliation plan requiring an additional $2.2 billion in cuts.[45] Much of its contents came from the Republican staff of affected committees.[46]

In this situation, incentives common to legislators became sharply manifest. Members seek to claim credit for government programs of assistance to their district[47] by reaching for the pork barrel.[48] Much of this effort is an attempt to protect the economic base of their districts, a politically essential concern for them.[49] Thus certain "swing" votes held by northeastern Republicans and southern Democrats could be had in return for the protection of benefits flowing back home.[50] As Democrat John Breaux (D-La.) so baldly put it when asked if his vote could be bought: "No, but it can be rented."[51] Southern Democrats received a second electoral benefit from their bargaining: if successful, they could vote for the president's program. "Many of us," according to Charles Stenholm (D-Tex.), "received a lot of pressure back home to support the president. For some it was overwhelming."

Stockman quickly discovered the boundaries of his reconciliation coalition. On one side were the Boll Weevils, who disliked big government but not when it aided the economies of their districts. As one Republican bargainer recalled: "But sure, we couldn't screw with TVA, Impact Aid, Farm programs; wouldn't cut a lot of dams. We had out eyes open, we knew what we had to do." On the other side were the Gypsy Moths, moderate northern Republicans who objected to harsh cuts in social and regional programs. Program preferences for allocational and redistributive projects back home would have to satisfied for any package to pass. The battle concerned the awarding of benefits through federal dollars, and this brought many more members aggressively into the process than any airy discussion of overall fiscal direction ever could.

The final result of such trading was, to David Stockman, a Pyrrhic victory in the House made worse by a conference in which the lower savings number was usually adopted in the final compromise reconciliation bill. Program politics vitiated the successful attainment of the Reagan spending strategy at the outset. As Stockman put it: "The borders of the American welfare state had been redefined, but they had only been slightly and symbolically shrunken from where they had stood before."[52] Perhaps, but the one-year savings were unprecedented—the compromise reconciliation bill required $35 billion in domestic cuts, four times the total of the 1980 reconciliation. Juxtaposing this fact alongside Stockman's assessment reveals the faulty political assumptions underlying the administration's fiscal strategy and tactics. He had assumed substantially more domestic cuts, and would not get them.

Congressional particularism also shaped the final form of the 1981 tax cut. The problem of controlling the reward of tax benefits, however, grew larger than that of imposing program cuts. The final bill reduced the revenue base of the federal government much more than the administration had proposed.[53] The original White House advocacy of Kemp-Roth and 10–5–3 gave way to accommodation of legislators' demands for special treatment of interests back home. Much of this was necessary to convince those skeptical of massive personal tax cuts to support the bill. Senator William Roth (R-Del.) recalled the problem: "Jack Kemp and I were mainly interested in reducing personal tax rates. All sorts of other things got added along the way in 1981." Senate Finance chair Robert Dole warned in May that without such changes the administration would not get the cuts it desired. An accommodation was reached by opening up the bill for additional pet revenue reductions.

Stung by the reconciliation defeat, the House Democratic leadership attempted to pass a rival version of the tax bill. Their alternative contained a plethora of special interest provisions while scaling back the personal and business cuts. The pivotal battle concerned the affections of the Boll Weevils, many of whom were skeptical of supply-side economics. In May, House Majority Leader Jim Wright reported that his conversations with fifty of the sixty-three Democrats who had voted for the Gramm-Latta resolution indicated that most agreed not to back the administration's tax proposals. "Very few of us," according to Buddy Roemer (then

D-La., later the Republican governor of that state) "were at all enthused about the supply-side cuts. Our final support for it was less than resounding." But an accommodation was reached with the administration through the rewarding of specific tax breaks. On July 29, forty-eight Democrats voted for the White House plan, thirty-six of them southern Democrats.

Conservative ideology forced an additional major change in the Senate. A favorite revenue initiative of some Senate Republicans was tax indexing, which would prevent the government from receiving a surge in revenues through inflation-spawned tax bracket creep, as it had in the 1970s. Thus a major allocational goal of conservatives—limiting tax revenue—would be achieved through this simple but extremely expensive change. The administration had hoped to delay indexing till later, but Dole and fellow Finance member Bill Armstrong (R-Colo.) saw the need to strike while the iron was hot. The change was argued on "good government" grounds. The government should not unfairly and secretly benefit in revenues from inflation; tax increases should be legislated. The Senate passed the indexing amendment by a 57–40 margin in late July. A conservative allocation goal was met, but at the eventual cost of burgeoning budget deficits—a steep drop in inflation beginning in 1983 produced a large decline in government revenues.[54]

After the tax conference, David Stockman confronted changes in law that cut taxes much more than he had planned and cut spending not nearly enough to avoid the prospect of large deficits.[55] The direction of economic argument had changed, and with it, the structure of the fiscal situation. Congress, desperate for innovative stabilization tactics, had ratified changes based on an unprecedented fiscal strategy. Tax cuts and less redistributive spending would transform expectations and resurrect the economy while defense spending underwent a historic peacetime increase. But this framework did not adequately acknowledge the political forces influencing legislative behavior on specific taxing and spending decisions. Congress was quite capable of adopting fiscal tactics in a resolution and undermining them in specific tax and spending bills. Partisanship as well as the political and ideological imperative of protecting programs and dispensing tax breaks had shrunk the revenue base to seventeen percent of GNP while not commensurately reducing spending.[56] The magnitude of this problem would become clear as economic growth slowed in the second half of 1981 while defense and Social Security spending steadily increased.

THEMES OF DEBATE

As the Reagan budget proposals dominated the legislative agenda, the administration's economic ideology defined the congressional debate. The sweeping White House plan raised basic questions of political economy—about the size of government, necessary and unnecessary programs, and how to improve economic performance—and 1981 witnessed its rhetorical success. The Reagan administration's supporters defined the problem and staked out the parameters of acceptable solution.

Democrats in the House and Senate, while critical of the administration's economic plans, conceded much to their opposition. First, most believed the role of government had to be reduced. As Leon Panetta (D-Cal.) admitted to David Stockman in a hearing of the House Budget committee: "I think on the cut side, frankly, you are headed in the right direction in terms of trying to get the deficit down, trying to get spending down. I think this is a direction that everybody recognizes we have to move in."[57] Second, many agreed that defense spending had to be increased. Carl Levin (D-Mich.), a liberal member of the Senate Armed Services committee, claimed on the floor that the American public is "willing to bear the cost of higher defense expenditure, which I believe they need, because security is the most basic human need."[58] Third, most acknowledged that tax cuts in some form were necessary to stimulate the economy. Ernest Hollings, ranking member of the Senate Budget committee, argued on the floor that "President Reagan and this Congress and the people of this country are in agreement on spending cuts. They are in agreement on cutting regulations. They are in agreement, Mr. President, on increasing defense, and they are in agreement on tax cuts."[59] Various liberal amendments to the budget resolution took exception only to specific aspects of this consensus.[60]

The commonly employed pejorative adjective used against the administration's program was "unfair," as in this declamation against Gramm-Latta I by Representative Matt McHugh (D-N.Y.):

"The spending cuts it proposes are unfair, falling especially hard on the most vulnerable in our society. Consider these examples [mentions of specific education, job-training, and economic development program cuts]. . . . Finally, the president's tax proposal is unfair and based on a faulty premise. It is unfair because under Kemp-Roth, most of the benefits would go to upper-income Americans."[61] At the root of the objections of many Democrats lay distributive preferences. Republicans responded to such charges by referring to the administration's claim of the preservation of the "social safety net," a group of programs exempt from cuts in the administration plan, including Social Security, Medicare, veteran's benefits, Supplemental Security Income, youth summer jobs, and low-income school lunches.[62]

But it was the prospects for stabilizing the economy that became the main subject of discussion in both chambers. The scale of the proposed fiscal change compelled members to address both its theoretical premises and short-term economic consequences. Some Democrats claimed disaster would ensue because the administration had deluded itself by adopting falsely optimistic assumptions about the program's effect upon the economy. Representative Stan Lundine (D-N.Y.) on the House floor charged the administration's budget was "disqualified as truly conservative. To understand why, one need only examine its economic assumptions. . . . No one should doubt that unrealistic economic assumptions can have a devastating impact."[63] Ernest Hollings began debate on the first resolution by berating the budget committee majority for adopting OMB assumptions (as had Gramm-Latta I in the House) and mentioning uncertainty in the financial markets over the administration plan by reading headlines from the *Wall Street Journal* and other business publications. To Hollings, "the resolution cannot be a credible statement of our fiscal policy for the next three years unless it is based on realistic economic assumptions. It is that credibility which the economy desperately needs."[64]

A common thread of Democratic criticism held that the tax cuts would be inflationary. Quotations from prominent economists (such as Lester Thurow of MIT and Walter Heller of Minnesota) and Wall Street oracle Henry Kaufman appeared repeatedly in support of this argument. Senator Bill Bradley (D-N.J.) explained the logic of this approach: "If you take one side of the ledger and put budget cuts and put on the other side the tax cuts and the increased defense expenditures, you end up with over $100 billion in fiscal stimulants. . . . There is a school of economics that would argue that when you have $100 to $120 billion excess fiscal stimulants, you are going to have a little inflation; that means higher interest rates and that means slower economic growth. If you do that, it is going to have that impact."[65] Demand-side effects would prevail.

Keynesian economists argued such consequences would result, and many Democrats relied upon them in developing a stabilization critique of Reaganomics. Representative Thomas Downey (D-N.Y.) during a Budget committee hearing went so far as to read to Murray Weidenbaum, chair of the Council of Economic Advisors, a series of quotes critical of the administration's policy from economists Downey identified as Keynesian—Otto Eckstein, Robert Samuelson, Gardner Ackley, and Henry Aaron.[66]

But using Keynesian economists for critical firepower by no means meant Democrats endorsed the traditional stabilization strategy of employing the fiscal stimulants of public spending and tax cuts to those of low-income as an alternative to Reaganomics. Few publicly held to that creed in 1981. Explicit references to Keynes and his theories seldom issued from Democratic lips. James Jones even tried to discredit the administration program on the House floor by labeling it Keynesian: "The Kemp-Roth tax bill would in effect be a Keynesian consumption-oriented tax policy. It would stimulate demand, there is no doubt about it. . . . Does the United States need a stimulus to demand right now? I submit we do not."[67]

One could better stabilize the economy, according to leading moderates and liberals, by targeting a larger proportion of the tax cuts at business. James Jones had urged this; even liberal Representative David Obey (D-Wis.) argued at a Budget committee hearing that investment could be stimulated more efficiently if a tax program "provided more of the total tax relief to business and less to high income consumers."[68] Daniel Patrick Moynihan (D-N.Y.) sought to amend the revenue total of the Senate budget resolution to a level consistent with tax cut legislation passed by the Finance committee in 1980 that had provided half of its relief to business, a higher percentage than the Reagan administration had proposed.[69] Democrats by 1981 had joined the search for efficient ways to stimulate supply.

The Democratic stabilization strategy called for a little less of everything Reagan wanted to do. Less "unfairness," smaller tax cuts more targeted at business, more gradual defense increases—more cautious policy. The degree that Democrats shifted to the right in budget debates in 1981 can be overstated. Their approach was quite similar to the "fiscal caution" the Democratic Congress of 1979 and 1980 sought to pursue. This time, however, their ranks were reduced and they confronted an enthusiastic and numerous opposition.

Republicans in 1981 first disagreed with Democrats over the "practical theory" about the roots of the problem. Representative Thomas Bliley (R-Va.) spoke for many fellow partisans when he claimed:

> The history of our economic illness is quite clear. The federal government is the culprit. Under the guise of social progress, the federal government has, for the last thirty years, subjected the American people to runaway taxation and runaway regulation. These policies have produced back-to-back years of double digit inflation for the first time since World War I; interest rates of 15 percent and 7½ percent unemployment.[70]

This definition is straightforward compared to the various and convoluted Democratic explanations for the economic morass.[71] For most Republicans, reducing taxes would, in the words of Representative Virginia Smith (R-Nebr.), "reduce the rising burden on taxpayers, stimulate savings and investment, and provide incentives for productivity."[72] As Republicans had been saying for years, a smaller government would mean less inflation and more economic growth.

To Democratic complaints about unrealistic economic assumptions, Republicans replied with a simple sort of expectations theory. Dan Coats (R-Ind.) argued in the House that "we speak too much of numbers, statistics, projections, dollars, spending levels, and economic assumptions. We speak too little of how to restore confidence and hope for the future."[73] House Budget committee member Ed Bethune of Arkansas held that "only one of these programs can alter expectations and break the inflationary mindset that is ruining our economy. Only one can change behavior of the people with respect to how they work, produce, and invest."[74] Not all conservatives enunciated such visionary sentiments. Phil Gramm counseled against optimistic economic assumptions, arguing that both the House Budget committee and administration forecasts were "wrong." The real issue for him was "the reconciliation language." Gramm-Latta I had reconciliation instructions requiring binding cuts, unlike the committee resolution. Shooting with "real bullets" was the only way to bring spending under control. The resolution vote, then, was about spending restraint, not tax cuts.[75] More traditional fiscal conservatives like Gramm went along for the spending cuts, and planned more later.

Occasionally an economically sophisticated GOP legislator would wade into the stabilization thicket to dispute Keynesian economics. Republican Clarence Brown of Ohio, a member of the Joint Economic committee, argued that supply-side tax policy need not be inconsistent with monetary restraint, an important linkage in the administration's argument: "An important concept not used by demand-oriented Keynesian economists is that fiscal policy can be split. . . . A gradual reduction in the rate of growth of the money supply and a tight federal spending posture can be used to attack inflation. At the same time, tax cuts, carefully drafted to stimulate work effort, saving, and investment can be used to fight unemployment."[76] Economic events of the 1980s have supported the possibility of segmented fiscal policy effects, as the simultaneous low inflation and growth of 1983–85 suggests.[77] But the recession of 1981–82 hardly indicated that pronounced disinflation and growth could occur simultaneously. Few lawmakers concerned themselves with theoretical possibilities of this sort during the tumult of 1981.

But a vogue was established. The proper course required stimulus of supply, not consumption. With this woolly consensus as the strategy, political forces caused the administration plan to become the chosen tactic. Democrats either supported an approach based on similar principles (the House Budget committee product) or relied upon the nostrums of the economic liberalism of the late

1970s.[78] Neither could dislodge the momentum behind the administration's scheme.

WHY IT HAPPENED: IDEOLOGY AND POLITICS

The political nexus of the budget shift of 1981 involved the economic ideology of legislators and the political forces pressing fiscal demands on Congress. The numbers had changed: more conservatives, whose policy views and those of their constituencies pushed them strongly in the administration's direction, inhabited the House and Senate in 1981. The perception of a 1980 electoral mandate also worked in the president's favor. Darrell West's survey of 253 House offices in 1981 discovered that supporters of the president on Gramm-Latta I and II and the tax cut did so because they (1) believed the program would stimulate the economy, (2) perceived the president to have a popular mandate, (3) felt a need to respond to district opinion and had activist support in their districts for the plan.[79]

Disaggregating the pattern helps to explain the variety of decision-making situations. Most legislators simply did not encounter a dissonance of goals when voting on the administration bills. Republicans faced a clear "field of forces"—personal ideology (conveniently rationalized to accept certain vagaries of the Reagan plan), the supporting electoral coalition, and D.C. influences—pressing them to endorse the White House on key votes. Many Democrats faced comparable fields pushing them in precisely the opposite direction. West finds that on the tax cut vote, for example, "Supporters were more likely to have cited policy motivations, district pressures, and a Reagan mandate. Opponents, on the other hand, perceived no mandate and did not believe the tax cut would make good policy."[80]

The central players in the key votes of 1981, however, were the Boll Weevils. It was they who faced dissonant goals: reelection (district opinion) versus reduction of their influence in Washington (the possibility of reprisals by party leaders) and, with the tax vote, their own ideological reservations. West finds that although they shared ideological sympathies with the White House on spending cuts, many decided their votes on Gramm-Latta I and II at the last minute: "These people, by nature of their ideological commitment, should have made up their minds earlier in the process. The fact that Boll Weevils as a group were the latest deciders implies that short-term perceptions were critical to their vote choices."[81] Constituency pressures, West finds, in the form of mail and telephone calls, had substantial impact on their votes.[82] All of the twelve Boll Weevil Representatives I interviewed attested to the importance of constituency influences in 1981; influence with party leaders seemed to them a less compelling goal. Given a Democratic alternative, they nevertheless pressed themselves to Reagan. In so doing they satisfied their ideological predilections and constituents' desires simultaneously on Gramm-Latta I and II. Constituent demands overrode any ideological compunctions on the tax vote.

Congress endorsed the new direction not on the basis of a fundamental reconceptualization of the role of the national government in fiscal policy, but as a result of a few votes at the margin strongly influenced by short-term political forces.[83] Distributional and allocational choices in 1981 favored the crucial Boll Weevil element of the winning coalition. All this occurred because Congress was willing to gamble on stabilization in the context of a mood of skepticism about overall government size (macroallocation) that had evolved in the late 1970s. Times were so bad that desperation seemed appropriate.

What, then, had Congress prepared itself for in 1981? No new orthodoxy had replaced the now unfashionable use of Keynesian concepts. Supply-side was an improvisation, accepted as a short-term tactic because of presidential and constituency pressures. Entrenched member preferences on specific programs and on the role of equity in governmental taxation and spending had to be confronted in future fiscal actions. So without a consensus on future stabilization strategy, but with strong allocation and distribution views, the legislature embarked on an economic experiment. What of the practical theory on which it was based? That involved administration economic assumptions, to be disproved as false in the second half of the year. With firm views on parts of the budget, but no realistic picture of the economic future or clear consensus on how to stabilize the economy, Congress lurched ahead.

Congress in 1981 temporarily accepted a new fiscal philosophy as a context for policy choice. But within that context, budgets and tax bills were patched together in the same old way. This paradox launched a new fiscal era, one characterized not by acceptance of a new discipline derived from adherence to a strategy of fiscal restraint and supply-side stimulus, but by the stubborn persistence of traditional ways of budgeting. The administration refused to accept this reality; those ways of budgeting had to be assaulted by deficits, if necessary. An era of stalemate began.

CHAPTER 4

Sources of Stalemate 1982–1984

By late 1981, Congress was beset by three obstacles that would impede its ability to correct deficits in future years. It first was not at all clear what the appropriate stabilization strategy should be. What level of deficit reduction would be appropriate and over what time period? The economy already seemed headed for recession. Would this be the time for budget austerity? Second, legislators wanted to uphold their personal and constituent preferences about allocation and distribution. Could such desires be reconciled with whatever broader stabilization task might be necessary? The possibility grew more remote of finding a deficit solution that was positive-sum politically or in terms of policy. To act was now more likely to offend legislators' own program desires (bad policy) and those of their constituents (bad politics). Third, the intransigence of the president on fiscal issues made creating any policy politically quite difficult. After 1981 lawmakers encountered threats to cherished programs, a stabilization consensus consisting only of the vague injunction to lower the deficit, and a president who would raise the political costs of most actions they sought to take.

The fiscal problem was substantial, for several reasons. A sharp recession in 1981–82 boosted spending for income security. Stagflation from 1979 to 1983 pushed Social Security spending from 4.3 percent to 5.2 percent of GNP, producing a funding crisis for the system. Certain spending that predated Reagan contributed as well. Defense spending increases from the late Carter presidency (1979 and 1980) began to appear as outlays; not until 1983 did Reagan's defense initiatives actually show up as spending outlays. The tax cuts of 1981 also contributed. Even after tax increases in 1982 and 1984, an estimated $50 billion of the 1985 deficit resulted from the 1981 tax cuts. Overall, net interest costs increased dramatically because the government had to borrow more as deficits increased. Inflation followed by recession created "first an insistence by leaders on higher rates and then a great need to borrow," complicating the government's interest rate problem.[1] What to do? As the economy began to slump in late 1981, many lawmakers sought to defend programs sending dollars back home—counter-cyclical tactics of long standing. But as the economy resuscitated in 1983, the political stratum called for deficit reduction. But by then, public demands for particular deficit-reducing measures were practically nonexistent. The 1981 chorus for cuts was to be proved an aberration.

Though confronted with unprecedented deficit numbers and no mandate for particular actions to take to reduce them, legislators nevertheless did not sit on their hands.[2] In 1982, a $98 billion tax increase over three years passed and received a reluctant signature from the president. A smaller-scale tax hike and deficit reduction "down payment" gained approval in 1984. Congress tended to delude itself about the scope of its actions, though, in order to secure their passage. Table 4–1 illustrates congressional inaccuracy

TABLE 4–1   Congressional Assumptions and Economic Results 1982–85

	Fiscal year	Budget resolution[1]	Actual results	Difference
Real GNP	1982	2.3	−1.7	−4.0
growth[2]	1983	4.5	6.1	+1.6
	1984	4.7	4.7	—
	1985	4.1	2.5	−1.6
Inflation[3]	1982	10.4	4.5	−5.9
	1983	6.9	3.3	−3.6
	1984	5.0	3.6	−1.4
	1985	5.0	3.2	−1.8
Revenues	1982	657.8	617.7	−40.1
(in billions)	1983	665.9	600.6	−65.3
	1984	679.6	666.5	−13.1
	1985	750.9	734.1	−16.8

[1] Economic and revenue assumptions of the final conference report of the first budget resolution for the fiscal year.
[2] Real growth in GNP for the fiscal year.
[3] Change in the Consumer Price Index for the fiscal year.
Sources: Congressional economic assumptions complied by Mark Kamlet, Carnegie-Mellon University; revenue estimates from *Congressional Quarterly*; economic results from *Economic Report of the President, 1982–87*.

about the economic future in budget resolutions from 1981 to 1984. Optimistic growth estimates in 1982 and 1984 and inflation overestimates each year increased the projected revenues of the federal government much beyond what was actually collected.

Though legislators thought they were being "realistic at the time" (in the words of House and Senate Budget committee economists), adoption of such assumptions reduced the number of difficult spending and taxing choices necessary for hitting a "respectable" deficit target. Kamlet, Mowery, and Tsu discovered that congressional budget resolutions during this period featured rosier economic projections than those of CBO or OMB.[3] Senator Charles Grassley (R-Ia.) labeled this tendency an addiction to the "narcotic of optimism," but it also reflected the limitations of economic forecasting.[4] Congressional assumptions adopted from 1982 to 1984 were within the range of those offered by private forecasters, reflecting the limited accuracy of this enterprise.[5]

The "opening bid" of the White House consistently featured rosy projections that compounded difficulties for legislators. The president proposed budgets greatly out of balance and comprised of priority mixes that Congress did not accept—see Table 4–2. The legislature acceded to some defense increases but would not take the axe to nondefense spending. The White House nonetheless demanded domestic cuts in order to move toward balance, but never specified a multiyear deficit reduction plan that would achieve the goal, even according to its own optimistic estimates. Allen Schick notes that "once the deficit became entrenched, the president was not inclined to do much about it. He was convinced that tax increases enacted to reduce the deficit would generate additional expenditures instead, and he preferred to have a smaller government with a bigger deficit than a bigger government with a smaller deficit."[6]

In the midst of political hiatus, legislators received a substantial array of analysis and advice on fiscal policy. As one Senate Budget committee member put it, Congress was "swamped with experts, information, and explanations." Given White House pronouncements, members were forced to search on their own for a conceptual framework that would explain the fiscal problem. Congress found itself in a multiyear seminar on the complex question of the economic effects of the deficits, a sort of required course in

TABLE 4–2 Administration Proposals and Spending Results 1982–85

	1982 Admin. proposal[1]		1982 Results		1983 Admin. proposal		1983 Results		1984 Admin. proposal		1984 Results		1985 Admin. proposal		1985 Results	
	$	%[2]	$	%	$	%	$	%	$	%	$	%	$	%	$	%
Defense outlays	188.8	+19.9	185.3	+17.7	221.1	+19.3	209.9	+16.9	245.3	+16.9	227.3	+8.3	272.0	+19.7	252.7	+11.2
Nondefense outlays[3]	391.8	−7.9	443.2	+4.2	403.7	−8.9	471.0	+6.3	458.7	−2.6	470.6	−0.1	488.8	+3.9	514.8	+9.4
Defense budget authority	226.3	+25.7	216.5	+20.3	263.0	+21.5	245.0	+13.2	280.5	+14.5	265.2	+8.2	313.4	+18.2	294.7	+11.1
Nondefense budget authority[3]	431.4	−8.3	476.2	+1.2	406.0	−14.3	515.6	+8.3	475.1	−7.8	530.9	+3.0	528.5	−0.4	600.6	+13.1
Interest on public debt	114.7	+20.1	117.2	+22.7	132.9	+0.9	128.6	+9.7	144.5	+12.4	153.8	+19.6	164.7	+7.1	178.8	+16.3

[1]From the original administration budget request to Congress; i.e., 1984 numbers are from the February 1983 request. All totals in the table are in nominal dollars.

[2]Percentage change from previous year's budget totals in these categories.

[3]Includes all nondefense functional categories, income from federal loans, allowances, and undistributed, offsetting receipts.

Sources: Administration proposals from the *Congressional Quarterly Almanac*; results from Office of Management and Budget, *Historical Tables FY1988* (Washington: Government Printing Office, 1987).

practical theory and stabilization concepts. Not all were willing students, because the subject appeared impenetrable—the actual performance of the economy produced its share of confusions. As deficits increased, inflation declined, refuting the conventional wisdom of the late 1970s. Economic recovery persisted in 1983 and 1984 in spite of historically high real interest rates. For the political stratum, as well as budget captains and more thoughtful lawmakers, it was time to rethink their practical theories.

DEFICIT POLITICS FOR LEGISLATORS

An inspection of the *Congressional Record* from the years 1982 to 1984 yields hundreds of declamations concerning the "irresponsible" and "dangerous" fiscal course upon which the nation had embarked. Politically, members had to denounce such practices in order to appear responsible back home—as not part of the problem—and also to justify their deficit voting to themselves. In so doing they gradually learned a variety of reasons why deficits could be a stabilization disaster. At its basic "macro" level, the problem was clear-cut. Deficits had to be reduced. As White and Wildavsky note, "no side could say what the deficit should be," but Congress, at the behest of the political stratum, sought to find the answer anyway.[7]

The puzzle of the deficit total entailed another vexing problem. How to agree on an annual tactical package consistent with a multiyear deficit reduction strategy? In practical terms, in the words of a senior House Democrat, each annual budget round became an exercise in "taking hits or avoiding them." Each year the deficit would loom as undesirably large, the White House would propose an alternative that targeted its hits in a politically infeasible manner, effectively putting Congress on the spot. Where to cut? The incentive to defend constituency programs is well illustrated in the humorous give-and-take among Senate Budget committee members at a 1982 hearing:

> SENATOR RIEGLE: If we want to get these deficits down as I think we need to, we are going to have to take the ax to the sacred cows, and I am ready to do it.
> SENATOR DOMENICI: You are right. You just do not name the sacred cows, you name your sacred cows.

SENATOR METZENBAUM: . . . I would like to say to my good friend from Michigan that this table started to literally shake when you mentioned western water projects. Please do not do that any more.

SENATOR DOMENICI: We would balance the budget if we got rid of all western water projects.

SENATOR RIEGLE: It would help.

SENATOR DOMENICI: We will balance it by the year 4000 if we get rid of all of them [laughter].[8]

Senator John Tower (R-Tex.), chair of the Armed Services committee, played shrewdly upon the constituency maintenance imperative in an effort to protect the defense budget in 1983: "In anticipation of the defense cuts called for by so many members, I recently sent a letter to each Senator asking that he or she provide me with a list of programs in his or her state that could be reduced without any adverse impact upon national security. To date, I have received only six responses."[9]

An equally risky course involved advocacy of tax increases. Besides their inherent unpopularity, raising taxes also required presidential assent, which became increasingly difficult to obtain after 1982. As Representative James Jones put it: "Even small tax increases were hard to come by. The president would be hostile and he could make political hay with that position. It is no wonder that Democrats in the House and Senate Republicans were not willing to take him on publicly about that." Why expose yourself politically and ideologically if more parochially-minded members and the president may combine to defeat you? Such logic caused the budget battle to shrink into a contest of program priorities, while legislators gave lip service to a "too large" deficit.

A vivid example of such calculation lies in the 1983 Senate budget debate. Senator Sam Nunn (D-Ga.) spoke in favor of an alternative budget resolution he had cosponsored, but added a caution: "If we are going to have extremely high deficits, if none of the groups I have already identified is willing to take cuts, I shall choose my own priorities, as others will, and I shall vote for a higher number in defense when it gets down to the point of no hope for a balanced fiscal picture."[10] Senator Slade Gorton (R-Wash.) in that same debate summarized the problem: "Each member of this body has other values which conflict with the desire for lower budget deficits and often that conflict is won by one of those other values."[11] Similar difficulties beset the House. Budget committee member Marty Russo (D-Ill.) described the construction of resolutions as "a matter of trading off programs. The key ingredient in the process was finding a set of program spending totals that enough Democratic members could stomach, given the alternatives." Satisfying constituents was often a matter of "staving off attacks," in the words of Thomas Downey (D-N.Y.), also a member of the committee. "Good deficit reduction policy" became quite difficult to form into concrete proposals because of the problem of aggregating members' preferences in both chambers.

With lawmakers indefatigably striving to protect constituency interests, the strategically important arenas of fiscal battle varied with circumstances. In the Senate, each year brought new procedures and alliances as numerous budget proposals (known as "packages") and amendments received lengthy consideration on the floor. Though immersed in a procedural morass producing the rejection of eight alternative budget resolutions in 1982, the House in 1983 and 1984 was able to pass plans forged by the Democrats on the Budget committee that rivaled those of the Senate and administration. Consensus creation among House Democrats, however, was arduous. This was an arena in which potential political losses were high, lasting influence with peers could not be purchased easily and the incentives induced protection of particular aspects of spending and taxes, along with avoidance of blame for the broader deficit problem. Given this, it is impressive that Congress made any progress at all in deficit reduction in the three years after 1981.[12]

POLITICS AND PROCESS

The pattern of deficit politics grew drearily familiar in each of the three years after 1981. First, the administration would propose a budget that was pronounced "dead on arrival" in Congress due to its unrealistic spending cuts and optimistic economic assumptions. Second, a period of negotiation with the White House, sometimes involving congressional leaders from both parties and sometimes only Republicans, would seek to negotiate a compromise. Third, negotiations would either fail or produce a package that faced major alteration in Congress. Fourth, once Congress had acted, the result would be found to not produce the savings claimed because of rosy economic assumptions. The president then would intermittently veto spending bills, resulting in parts of the government shutting down for one day during three separate occasions during this period, and forcing Congress to relent some in the appropriations standoff. The deficits, meanwhile, persisted.

The legislature threatened to fragment from within in response to the contradictory pressures of deficit politics.[13] To compound the ordeal, agreement with the White House ultimately was necessary for any deficit reduction package. Table 4–2 shows Congress did accommodate the administration desire for defense increases to an extent, but balked at implementing the nondefense spending reductions the White House urged. Table 4–3 reveals the legislature's success in pressing revenue increases upon a reluctant White House. Overall, Congress from 1982 to 1986 cut domestic spending by five percent; most deficit reductions during this time came from tax increases and defense cuts.[14] Despite this limited consensus, deficits hovered near $200 million during the later years of Reagan's first term. Why? Economic and technical assumptions made during each year's deficit reduction usually provided the bulk of the supposed savings, and they were often wrong.[15]

If the White House was at best reluctantly pliable in this situation, so was the House Democratic leadership, particularly after Democrats gained 26 House seats in the 1982 elections. The 1981 defeat and subsequent economic downturn caused them to entrench further their program fortifications. In the words of one senior House Democrat, the leadership had as its major priorities in the budget fight "less for defense and a defense of social programs, most particularly Social Security." That program, with its millions of voting claimants and vociferous public defenders such as Representative Claude Pepper (D-Fla.), became a fiscal front upon which House Democrats waged a successful offensive in the early 1980s. One House Republican leader summed it up by saying that "for most of our members, altering Social Security benefits in any way became out of bounds." As Trent Lott, House Republican whip, stated to David Stockman in September 1981, when the administration was contemplating reductions in benefits: "Social Security is dead in the water. That's like in: No way! Period! End of

TABLE 4–3   Presidential Tax Proposals and Congressional
Enactments 1981–84 (billions of 1982 dollars)

	Proposals		Enactments		Difference	
	First year[1]	Fully effective[2]	First year	Fully effective	First year	Fully effective
1981	−56.6	−129.8	−37.7	−150.0	18.9	−20.2
1982	none		18.0	51.8	18.0	51.8
1983	none		none			
1984	none		10.6	22.5	10.6	22.5

[1]Expected revenue change first full year after law was passed.
[2]Expected revenue change in first full year that law is effective, if different from the first column. Note that the totals for congressional tax increases mentioned in the text refer to the projected revenue increase over the first three years that the law was in effect, as estimated at the time of passage. Hence the different totals than those included in this table. Source: Paul E. Peterson, "The New Politics of Deficits," in *The New Direction in American Politics* edited by John E. Chubb and Paul E. Peterson (Washington: Brookings Institution, 1985), p. 381. Reprinted by permission of the publisher.

discussion! Not a prayer!"[16] Some Republican members objected to cuts in principle, but most could see that it threatened electoral losses. House Republicans would not endorse any significant cuts in Social Security after 1981; Jack Kemp even urged the House Budget committee in 1982 to move the program off budget so that it not be subject to fiscal politics.

House GOP reticence did not prevent Pete Domenici from pressing for benefit reductions in 1981 and 1982. "At the time, there seemed no other way to solve a terrible problem other than through comprehensive restraint, and that included Social Security," he recalled. Domenici was unable to muster support in the Senate Budget committee in late 1981 for cuts. The White House did support his 1982 effort to reduce benefits by $40 billion over three years, which passed the committee on a 12–8 party-line vote. The proposal failed on the floor, in the face of Democratic denunciations of its unfairness. Minority Leader Robert Byrd termed it "mortgaging the economic future of the elderly to finance the economic folly" of the Reagan tax cuts.[17] A 1983 bipartisan reform of the long-term financial health of the program trimmed certain retirement benefits and delayed cost-of-living adjustments (COLAs) for six months. This removed the immediate financing threat to the program and also helped to insulate it from deficit politics.[18]

If reductions in Social Security and defense—20 percent and 26 percent of annual spending, respectively—were not seriously contemplated, what was left to cut? Other domestic spending was a possibility, but reconciliation on the revolutionary 1981 scale was not to be found on Capitol Hill during the subsequent three years. Congress failed to pass any reconciliation bill in 1983, and those of 1982 and 1984 did not again assault the authorization levels of the dozens of domestic programs hit in 1981. John Palmer has estimated that only $26 billion was saved during FY 83–86 through reductions in discretionary domestic spending, cuts totaling less than five percent of total domestic expenditure during that period.[19] Where did the savings come from? From reform of other entitlements, most significantly Medicare, and from the 1983 Social Security reform.[20] These reductions alone did not bring the budget close to balance. Once the administration's drive for domestic spending reductions stalled, the necessary spending cuts were not politically "doable."

Stalemate was accompanied by an elaborate "high politics" of negotiations between the administration and congressional leaders each year. The machinations in Congress accompanying this usually vain search for an executive-legislative compromise were complex indeed. Several reasons account for the Byzantine quality of stalemate politics. First, differing partisan control of the House and Senate after 1982 effectively put Senate Republicans in the middle, "working between the president and the Democratic House in the search for a solution," in the words of Senator Slade Gorton. This produced, in Gorton's words, "years of living dangerously" as Republican budget captains in the Senate tried in vain to sell tax increases to a skeptical administration and domestic spending cuts to a suspicious House. Senate Republicans enjoyed only limited success because the president and House leadership substantively disagreed with various of their initiatives and would not fully trust the senators. The House viewed them across a partisan and cameral divide; the administration did not believe it could always rely upon them to deliver Senate support for compromises and thus politically protect the president.

Within each chamber, budget leaders also faced the daunting

task of assembling the Appropriations, Budget, and taxation committees behind the implementation of a budget plan. Appropriations handled discretionary spending; tax committees revenues and entitlements. Any solution had to include an accommodation among these three, as well as between chambers and between the Congress and the administration. This required the Budget committees, in pursuit of a passable resolution, to defer in various ways to the interests of other committees and to any concordat reached with the administration. In 1982 the Budget committees ratified tax committee actions by providing for a $98 billion tax increase in the budget resolution. In 1984 the Senate Budget committee endorsed a "rose garden agreement" between Senate Republican leaders and the president, and both Budget committees included in their resolutions revenue increases forged by the tax committees.[21]

The perils resulting from an absence of accommodation surfaced in 1983 when the Senate passed a resolution asking for entitlement reforms and spending reductions unacceptable to the Appropriations and Finance committees. The committees failed to comply with the resolution after it was revised in conference, and no reconciliation bill passed at all. One senior Senate Budget staffer recalled: "The 1983 resolution was an absolute disaster. It was unenforceable. The Senate should have known when it passed that the committees would stall it. A huge mistake." At a less celebrated level, accommodation to the interests of other committees remained the rule of the day in crafting budget resolutions. Members of taxation and Appropriations panels sit on the Budget committees of both chambers and unashamedly claim the protection of the prerogatives of their "home" committees as part of their job.[22]

The budget process had to twist and bend to adapt to these numerous institutional pressures in 1982, 1983, and 1984. The second budget resolution was scrapped after 1981 because of the difficulties in agreeing twice in one year on awful aggregates. Instead, the totals of the first resolution became binding on October 1, and then were revised to accord with economic events and spending pressures during the ensuing fiscal year. Congress missed the May 15 deadline for the first resolution each year, completing it in late June in 1982 and 1983, but not in 1984 until the first day of FY 1985. The House in 1983 and 1984 debated and passed appropriations bills in advance of a conference agreement on a budget resolution. The Budget committees often had to grant waivers to conformance with a nonexistent resolution in order for the appropriations process to proceed. The pace of appropriations business also slowed because of delays in reaching budget accord. Continuing resolutions had to be passed to cover spending for nine of the thirteen annual appropriations bills in 1983 and 1984.[23]

To summarize: take an unprecedented problem—persistent, large deficits—with unknown but possibly drastic economic effects, combine with a rigid adminstration committed to a politically infeasible approach to the problem, and a bevy of legislators possessing deeply rooted preferences about programs that cannot be aggregated into a fiscal solution in the absence of presidential leadership. Augment this with a partisan division between the two chambers and the convoluted process of reaching consensus within each chamber among the mutually suspicious committees concerned with taxing, spending, and budgeting. The result? A situation in which most solutions appear to legislators to be policy and political losers. That limited progress could occur is perhaps the most one could expect of congressional political economy. Stabilization strategy was at best loosely defined and politics prevented annual tactical decisions adequate to solve the problem. The threat of deficits helped Congress to move haltingly toward deficit reduction, dragging the president and its more parochially minded members reluctantly along. It was a situation in which the fiscal actions of many legislators would seem increasingly dissonant with their expressed goal of deficit reduction.

THINKING IT THROUGH

After the fall of supply-side from vogue, Congress had to comprehend the onset and likely impact of deficits. Administration analysis was suspect, and opinions among economists were variable, as usual. Public and expert opinion—the political stratum—counseled in favor of deficit reduction, but widely disputed the specific consequences of deficits for the economy. The challenge was to reformulate practical theories about the economy and, for more thoughtful members, revise and adjust personal ideology accordingly. But the allocative and distributive program preferences of most in Congress would yield only slightly under the pressure of events. The tension lay squarely between deficit reduction and program defense. Scapegoating as a means of dissonance reduction appeared in force on the House and Senate floors. Democrats blamed the Reagan administration for deficits, Republicans the Carter administration.

Alongside such acrimony, interpretations of the effects of deficits evolved gradually over this period; as the red ink persisted, so did a diversity of views about its consequences. Accompanying this discourse were traditional arguments about the size of government and propriety of redistribution. Congress had to relate the new economic situation to long-standing views about the proper fiscal role of government. Budget debates disclosed how members individually and collectively puzzled their way through the task.

The administration had its own response to the deficit era, which it routinely repeated in each budget proposal. Its arguments became the conservative pole of Washington fiscal argument in the first half of the 1980s. According to the president, deficits resulted from unnecessary domestic spending: "These deficits reflect the excess spending commitments of the past rather than new spending programs. . . . The federal budget was drastically overcommitted in nondefense areas if the federal tax take was to be restored to levels compatible with strong economic growth."[24] This combined with rapid disinflation and the cyclical downturn of 1982 to exacerbate the problem. In confronting economic difficulties, the administration's allocative and distributive positions budged not at all. Defense increases were always "necessary" to strengthen national security. The best domestic policy was economic growth induced by lower deficits. Lower deficits could be achieved through reductions in unnecessary spending programs such as Amtrak and legal services for the poor. The budget was to be balanced at a lower percentage of GNP.[25]

Though this opening bid did succeed in placing Congress on the defensive, the White House failed to make tactically feasible its long-term strategy for transforming allocation, distribution and stabilization. The administration from 1982 to 1984 did not propose a budget that came close to balance in any year projected by its calculations. With defense, taxes, and eventually Social Security off limits, the central problem for David Stockman after 1981 was "identification of a gigantic layer of fat in this small budget remainder." It was not there. "Not a trace of this huge mysterious layer of waste can be found in recently proposed administration budgets,"[26] wrote Stockman in 1986. The White House always proposed greatly unbalanced budgets because the range of cuts they would countenance was too small to fill the gap and substantial tax increases were forbidden.

Congress of course rejected the rudiments of the administration approach in the three years after 1981. The legislative "mainstream" held that substantial tax increases had to be considered, domestic spending could not and should not be cut substantially below the level of 1981, but defense growth could be slowed down. Congress actually increased job program spending in 1982 as a small gesture of relief for victims of the recession. The national government had to move toward budget balance, but not at the low level of GNP proposed by the administration and not with the allocation and distribution mix embodied in administration budget proposals. The basic problem, of course, remained: How to agree to a deficit reduction course that would not be negative-sum both politically and in terms of policy? The dissonance of goals was unavoidable. Even though agreement existed in Congress on a general strategic direction for stabilization, consensus on a specific proposal was not forthcoming. Presidential intransigence and all sorts of ideological and constituency concerns impeded that progress.

The mainstream was not the sole stream, however; differing bodies of opinion arose within the legislature. Republicans as a whole tended toward the administration's analysis, but often drew a line in defense of specific spending programs. Only a vociferous minority, including Jack Kemp in the House and a faction of hard-core conservatives in the Senate, continued to promote a supply-side perspective. Southern Democrats wanted stricter spending controls than their partisan colleagues from other regions of the country, but like them looked askance at supply-side doctrine promising a "growth dividend" as a means to budget balance. To them, liberal Democrats were soft on spending control, while Republicans ignored the reality of defense waste. Buddy Roemer presented a Boll Weevil alternative budget resolution in 1984, mandating a two percent across-the-board cut in spending, arguing: "Growth alone without tax reformation, growth alone without nondefense discipline, growth alone without reining in the generals will not solve the deficit problem. . . . We should cut the military back, freeze domestic spending, and trim entitlements slightly."[27] As Richard Ray of Georgia put it: "Southern Democrats were in between. Supply-side was discredited, but other members of our party were not vigilant enough on spending control." The increased Democratic majority in the House after 1982 made them less pivotal in budget deliberations, but many southerners found the resolutions crafted by Jones and the Budget committee to be sufficiently prudent fiscally to reward them with support. As one commented: "It was the best we could get, and we wanted to support the leadership if possible after the big showdown of 1981. Many of us realized the tax cuts helped to bring on the budget problem." A shared understanding of the cause of the deficit helped keep Democrats more united on budget resolutions in 1983 and 1984.

Roemer's "freeze" proposal was one of several attempts to transcend the standard allocation and distribution arguments that sidetracked debate over resolutions onto parts of the budget. The idea of freezing all spending across-the-board originated with Representative Denny Smith (R-Ore.) in late 1981, and was quickly adopted by Senator Ernest Hollings. To Hollings an overarching norm of "equal treatment" was necessary to rise above squabbles over priorities: "This approach is fair. It means that government as well as the private sector and all elements of society would share in the sacrifice necessary to turn the economy around. The essential ingredient on this approach must be fairness. If we abandon that principle, we will not be able to prevail."[28] The principle grew popular, but politicians differed tremendously over its concrete application. By 1983 and 1984, all sorts of "freeze" proposals were floating around the Hill. The administration argued "fairness" in proposing a domestic spending freeze in 1983. In the Senate, Joseph Biden (D-Del.), Nancy Kassebaum (R-Kan.), and Charles Grassley (R-Iowa) urged adoption of a freeze package in 1983 and 1984. Hollings also routinely proposed one, sometimes in tandem with Senators Mark Andrews (R-N.D.) and J. James Exon (D-Nebr.).

None passed, because they treated too crudely the program preferences needing careful political balance in budget resolutions and did little to quell the sharp ideological divisions rising in a legislature under fiscal pressure. Growing deficits and a common belief in the urgency of the problem led to the pursuit of villains; long-established partisan arguments over government size and re-distribution regularly surfaced in budget debates. Democrats would routinely assault Republican unfairness, and Republicans would counter with arguments about deficits produced by waste-ful domestic spending. Freeze proposals calmed such waters not at all.[29]

Fiscal imbalance did produce new lines of division over defense spending. Some southern Democrats sought to rein in Pentagon increases sought by the administration. Certain Republicans began to doubt the efficacy of large defense increases as well. House Budget committee member Bud Shuster (R-Pa.) stated at a hearing in 1983: "I have been called a hawk on defense, and I guess that is true, but the administration's defense increases are just too high."[30] Senator Charles Grassley became so exercised about Pen-tagon waste that he lost no opportunity to argue in favor of freez-ing the defense budget in 1983 and 1984.[31] Such criticisms met with a stalwart response from conservative members of the Armed Services committees and their sympathizers.[32] Given the pressures of the deficit, the rate of increase was scaled back after 1981—not as much as House Democrats desired, but more than Senate Re-publicans and the president preferred.

Alongside all these program-level vexations, the future of the economy loomed as the great imponderable in post-1981 budget discussions. Ernest Hollings summarized the confusion in 1983: "Everybody in this town has turned into an economist—incentive, stabilization, destabilizing, provocative, exacerbating, everything except the actual fact. We have gone amok."[33] Yet one problem became "privileged" in the minds of congressional budget captains and many other legislators: interest rates. Real rates hovered at or near historic highs in the first half of the decade. Though inflation fell to 3.2 percent in 1983, the prime rate averaged 10.79 percent; in 1984 prices rose 4.3 percent while the prime increased to 12.04 percent.

Representative Bill Archer (R-Tex.) spoke for many during a 1982 budget debate when he defined the primary economic threat: "That problem is interest rates. If we are honest, we must face the fact that interest rates today relative to inflation are the highest in the history of the United States of America. All of the other specific problems that have been mentioned previously in this debate cannot be solved if we do not get interest rates down."[34] Ranking Senate Budget committee Democrat Lawton Chiles of Florida echoed this rationale when discussing a budget resolution one year later: "The central issue before the Senate in this budget debate is interest rates. That is right—interest rates. The life of the economic recovery is tied to them. The ability of Americans to find work depends on interest rates: how low we can get them, and how many jobs will be produced as a result. . . . So, while we will talk about lots of issues in the days ahead, they will all come back to interest rates, and what we can do to bring them down and keep them down."[35]

Interest was economic topic number one. Most budget alternatives discussed on the House and Senate floor in the three years after 1981 were justified by their supposed effects in bringing interest rates down.[36] Why the focus on interest rates? The salience of interest rates lay in their national and local economic importance. For one, the political stratum and financial markets harped on it.[37] High rates, they claimed, threatened to choke off the nascent recovery of 1983 and keep the economy in a state of permanent recession. Constituents also had complaints. Rates affected the economic base of communities back home; businesses and borrowers suffered directly, stimulating legislators to find ways to help. Representative Charles Stenholm (D-Tex.) stated: "My farmers have to borrow, and interest rates are killing them." His House colleague Ralph Regula (R-Ohio) claimed that "rates are bad for business and consumers throughout my district and I sure hear about it." It is not surprising that the 1986 questionnaire revealed interest rates ranking high as an influence on the economy. Stabilization worries and constituency protection needs fused around this problem; addressing it became tactically imperative.

A related fear was the onset of a new bogey: the "structural deficit." By 1983, the term had entered the congressional fiscal lexicon. CBO defined it as a "standard employment deficit," "an estimate of how the deficit would look if the economy were strong enough to keep the unemployment rate at six percent."[38] All CBO and OMB projections in 1983 and 1984 showed the structural deficit growing steadily in future years. Even if the economy expanded steadily at a three percent rate and unemployment remained stable at six percent, the real and nominal levels of deficits would increase. Fiscally aware members took this as the real measure of the budget problem. As Representative James Jones put it: "When we on the Budget committee got wind of the structural deficit problem, it dramatized to us, and eventually to other members, that deficits wouldn't just melt away. We had to address the problem and not avoid it." Legislative explanations of the structural deficits were ideologically predictable; Democrats pointed to the 1981 tax cuts and increases in defense spending, Republicans reflected administration views in labeling domestic spending the problem.[39]

A "macro" fear grew among those in the political stratum that large and growing structural deficits would effectively "crowd out" private borrowers in capital markets and smother economic growth. The 1982–83 recession produced alarm for many in Congress who saw tight monetary policy by the Federal Reserve combined with large deficits producing high real rates even while the economy was slumping. House Budget committee member Richard Gephardt (D-Mo.) voiced concern in a hearing held in the middle of the downturn: "When you take the whole picture and look at it, what you wind up with is a massive conflict between fiscal and monetary policy which I think has caused high, high interest rates, which has aggravated our situation greatly."[40] High real rates continued, sustaining the fear of crowding out. A worry first voiced by Domenici in late 1981 was repeated by him in 1983: "There is an ever-present concern that as the economic recovery proceeds, growing private borrowing needs may collide with large federal borrowing and force interest rates even higher. This in turn could cut short the economic recovery and bring back stagflation."[41]

In fact, this did not happen. Instead, large inflows of foreign capital invested in Treasury securities allowed economic expansion to proceed apace alongside a large budget deficit in 1983 and 1984. In this way the sharp decline in dollar velocity in the early 1980s, though driving up the value of the dollar on international currency markets, did not "abort" recovery from recession.[42] The absence of an economic crunch served to perpetuate the political stalemate.

As the recovery began in 1983, the political stratum and budget captains claimed that high real interest rates contributed to
another growing problem: a rising trade deficit resulting from the
appreciating dollar. Lawton Chiles summarized the what had become conventional wisdom of Congress on this matter by 1984:
"The failure to address deficits will drive interest rates higher. The
deficit will force the dollar higher, and that means the trade deficits
are going to be higher, and that means that we are going to lose
more jobs. All these problems come back to the size of our deficits."[43] The high dollar damaged export-dependent sectors of the
economy, most notably agriculture, and those negatively affected
by influxes of imports, such as textiles. Legislators from these
regions spoke out strongly on the need to reduce the trade deficit,
the value of the dollar, and interest rates.[44]

Budget leaders in Congress continually sought to influence the
psychology of capital markets. As high rates persisted, legislators
of both parties tried to send a message that fiscal policy would be
brought under control, hoping to convince money managers to
reduce real rates and finally dispose of inflation fears spawned by
persistent deficits. James Jones referred to the president's fiscal
proposals in 1982: "Psychology is a very important factor in the
success or failure of this program, and a key psychological factor is
what the business community thinks of it."[45] Senator Paul Tsongas
(D-Mass.) remarked in 1984: "If Washington does not take the
deficit seriously, Wall Street does. Financial markets have been
unstable and nervous since the beginning of the year, waiting to see
what we in Washington will do."[46] Barber Conable commented in
the midst of a reconciliation debate that year: "Since this is a
psychological effort we are making to try to encourage people to
believe that we are serious about deficit reduction, the size of the
reconciled reduction is the important element to the markets,
which now are expressing great concern about our ability to face
up to the final issue."[47]

Budget policy was driven by the need to establish credibility
with the political stratum and business community in the hope of
nudging interest rates downward. But first a reputable source
would have to identify an adequate annual level of deficit reduction
for Congress to pursue. Prominent businesspeople and economists
were regularly quizzed on this at Budget committee hearings. The

views of Paul Volcker, chair of the Federal Reserve Board, carried particular weight. His 1984 target of $50 billion in deficit reductions became a serious goal mentioned by Republicans and Democrats in budget debates. Alongside ideological and constituent preferences, "market confidence" dominated the political economy of fiscal policy throughout the early eighties.[48] The problem was that no estimate was authoritative; each was only a guess. The administration had no clear deficit reduction target, nor did Democrats. And Volcker was one among many, perhaps a lead in the chorus but certainly not the choir director. Without such a director, no fiscal goal could be effectively established.[49]

THE FISCAL FACTIONS

The debate over what sort of fiscal policy was cyclically correct occurred in this muddled context—and differences abounded in Congress. Though most Republican budget alternatives sought to avoid major tax increases after 1982, significant differences over the appropriate fiscal course annually turned up in Republican ranks. The "pure" supply-side perspective arose from Jack Kemp in the House and a small group of "hard core" Republican Representatives (including Dreier of California, Hartnett of South Carolina, Courter of New Jersey, Siljander of Michigan, and Gingrich of Georgia) and Senators (including Helms of North Carolina, Mattingly of Georgia, Jepsen of Iowa, Humphrey of New Hampshire, Hatch of Utah, and Armstrong of Colorado). Their constant theme was the need to avoid tax increases of any sort.[50] Kemp differed from most other supply-side sympathizers in his resistance to large cuts in spending, believing that a strong economic recovery would bring the budget back to near balance. Others of the "hard core" were less convinced of this, but wanted reduced allocation anyway.

Senate Republican leaders found themselves in frequent cyclical arguments with their own right wing. Baker, Dole, and Domenici believed deficit reduction had to happen, and if it required additional revenues in 1982 and 1984, so be it. The primary problem for Pete Domenici was the clear and present danger of deficits to economic growth, making a compromise on immediate deficit reduction an absolute imperative: "It was a matter of reaching agreement on a package with many parts. We just had to have deficit reduction, and you had to be flexible in the components you put into your plan." The divergence among Republicans concerned both stabilization strategy and tactics; those on both sides of the issue thought their approach would be acceptable to constituents and to the markets.

If Republicans divided between hard-core and more moderate elements over taxes, Democrats lacked a common theme in their confusing response to stabilization problems after 1981. With the onset of the recession, some Democrats, like Jim Wright, urged a consumption-oriented tax cut, but gradually the view that tax increases were necessary to cut the deficit won out.[51] House Democrats in 1983 even contemplated eliminating the third year of personal tax cuts, though this would disproportionately penalize moderate and low income taxpayers, as Republicans delighted in pointing out. The House budget resolutions of 1983 and 1984, compromise documents built within the party, were fiscally cautious attempts to gradually move toward budget balance. With budget policy in such disarray, no bold redistributive or stabilization alternative could win consensus support in the party. Creating an annual fiscal austerity consensus was slow work.

Some distributive positions and stabilization tactics voiced by Democrats echoed the party's fiscal tradition, such as a proposal capping the total amount of the tax cut for individuals and the frequent excoriation of the Federal Reserve for its tight money during the 1981–82 recession. But the argument most often heard in their ranks was an indictment of the administration's fiscal excess in incurring large deficits. That Democrats became the party decrying the fiscal profligacy of the White House was rich in irony; this stance caused the Democrats to drop all pretenses to Keynesian justifications for deficits.[52] Democrats instead positioned themselves as the market-sensitive moderate alternative to Reaganism. Full-employment Keynesianism was at least temporarily vanquished by the size of the deficit problem. Few Democrats even seriously proposed such ideas.

What were, then, the Democratic party's strategy and tactics for economic stabilization from 1982 to 1984? As one Democratic representative put it: "less of the same—lower deficits—with pro-gramatic fairness, meaning less for defense and more for domestic." No grand stabilization theory guided them. The problem became a more finite one of assessing the business cycle and determining how to raise revenues without hurting expansion. Democrats effectively surrendered ideological ground in stabilization debate in order to pursue a politically acceptable solution to the deficit. Political acceptability meant that programmatic "fairness" could prevail for their constituents and the party could look fiscally responsible overall. Leon Panetta, a House Budget committee member and Democratic moderate, commented in late 1981: "I think if there's anything that Democrats have to learn, it's that we have to approach the economy in a disciplined sense, and we do not have that image." This meant accepting that deficits were bad, not that some might be defensible in Keynesian terms: "Like a rose, a deficit is a deficit is a deficit."[53]

All this was good news to southern Democrats in the House. Large deficits led them finally to abandon their flirtation with supply-side economics and become more receptive to tax increases. "You have to pay for what you buy, it's as simple as that," according to Marvin Leath. "We began to see the need for tax increases to close the deficit, the president and many Republicans did not." Of course, the southerners had lost much of their strategic importance in budget policy as a result of the Democratic gains in the 1982 House elections. It thus behooved them to make peace with a leadership less dependent upon them for support. Nevertheless, the orthodox fiscal conservatism they espoused placed deficits high on the list of horrors. Supply-side was a new wrinkle for them, deficit control was not. For political and ideological reasons, many could countenance the fiscally "moderate" resolutions of the House Budget committee. Only thirty of eighty-seven southern Democrats opposed the Budget committee resolution on the floor in 1983; only nineteen of eighty-three in 1984. Their greater loyalty made possible the triumph of Democratic budget resolutions, arduous House-Senate conferences, and protracted and often futile negotiations with the White House. Such were the frustrations of deficit politics.

CONCLUSION

The collapse of administration credibility, macroeconomic confusion over simultaneous deficits, recession, and disinflation, and the threat to programs could only serve to foster congressional inaction from 1982 to 1984. But the very scale of the fiscal problem produced an unmistakable rallying cry: reduce the deficit. This Congress did, with the reluctant assistance of the president. But it did not do it very much. The consensus strategy was vague and not carefully justified, based on a fear of interest rates and uncertain practical theories about the future economic course. Programmatic pressures were strong and immediate—ideology and constituency would guide any solution. An ambitious response by the Congress could make its members worse off in terms of their program preferences, but the correct sort of deficit reduction to inflict upon the economy was not so clear. Just what tactics to employ in solving the problem was a puzzlement, but it was clear that policy and political losses would be taken in any such attempt.

Lawmakers reduced their personal dissonance by claiming the fault lay elsewhere and in so doing they magnified certain differences among themselves. Entrenched ideological divisions permitted the ready identification of evil perpetrators whose poor allocation and distribution decisions had created the current budget problems. Democrats were accused of profligate domestic spending; Republicans of an excessive tax cut and defense buildup. This squabble did not clarify what Congress should be doing in this situation.

Democrats decided to "me-too" on deficit reduction as southerners, disillusioned with supply-side experiments, made common allocational cause with their more liberal brethren. The resulting party "consensus" involved demure tactics of slight deficit reductions, with all eyes on capital markets. Fiscal urgency declined with the onset of recovery, but rose as the 1984 elections neared. Congress found itself fine tuning in reference to immediate political and economic cycles—within the political limits of action, which were severe. The "big picture" was addressed variously during this time, but some more mundane constants of legislative life remained. The entrenched ideological-constituency preferences of legislators, alongside an improving economy and unresponsive White House, explains the timorous progress of 1982–84.

CHAPTER 5

Gramm-Rudman-Hollings and After

A cursory examination of deficit politics in Congress during the second half of the 1980s might produce the conclusion that the period was characterized by complexity, turmoil, and change. The formal budget process experienced all of this, but underlying the hullabaloo was a remarkable stability of perspective on the part of individual legislators. The basic features of lawmakers' decision environments that appeared during the onset of deficits after 1981 did not alter with the hurly-burly of events later in the decade. Elite and constituent opinion continued to oppose deficits, but the pro-spending or antitax opinions of legislators and their home supporters remained as strong as ever. One could accurately continue to claim not to be at fault and blame the deficits upon the actions of political opponents. Confusion over the economically appropriate size of annual deficit reduction remained. And the sky had not fallen—though elite opinion warned that it might any day, the immediate pressure for action to abrogate program commitments simply was not there. These conditions persisted throughout the decade, effectively scuttling the budget discipline of Gramm-Rudman-Hollings.

Events during 1985–89 give firm endorsement to the above theme, as this chapter will demonstrate. Gramm-Rudman-Hollings (hereafter GRH), though touted as a counter to program politics, gained its form and passage through those very politics. When GRH threatened established political relationships of lawmakers, it was brushed aside (with help, as we will see, from the courts). Only when economic events in 1987 brought immediate trouble to mind did the legislature and executive stir from their entrenched positions. When the problem seems primarily not to be your fault, but rather everybody's problem and everybody's fault, it is plausible to place blame first on one's enemies. That way business as usual can persist.

All this changed in 1990, one of the most consequential budget years since 1981. It did so not because of some fundamental transformation of congressional behavior, but because of a remarkable shift in presidential behavior. George Bush pushed hard for a multiyear package forcing major deficit reductions and for reform of the budget process in order to make spending control more firm. He persisted in his stance when the crunch came in October, even vetoing a temporary spending bill in order to shut down much of national government over a weekend. Bush also demonstrated a greater flexibility over the program specifics of the package than he or Ronald Reagan had in the past. The result was the largest deficit reduction agreement since 1981, and seemingly firm controls on spending for the duration of the five-year agreement. The political cost to Bush, however, was substantial. As prime mover in a controversial, divisive, and at times chaotic budget year, he saw his public approval drop some twenty points in opinion polls in the course of two months in the autumn of 1990. Congress acceded to Bush's initiative, but just barely, and only after a big fight about program specifics—the major impediment to resolution of the deficit problem throughout the decade. This persistence of disagreement over budget parts produced the frustration that propelled passage of Gramm-Rudman-Hollings in 1985.

THE MOUNTING FRUSTRATIONS OF 1985

By 1985 legislators could accurately claim that the votes they cast for deficits were not the result of personal culpability, but rather of a collective problem of aggregating disparate preferences within Congress in the face of executive intransigence. Though this argument might produce a modicum of personal comfort, it did little to reduce deficits. The red ink for FY 1986 would total $221 billion, a nominal record, and stand at 5.3 percent of GNP, quite sizeable for peacetime. After three years of nibbling at the deficit, the problem had not substantially abated, and frustration among lawmakers was reaching the boiling point. Pressure from the political stratum to "be responsible" remained strong. Senate Republicans had bitten the bullet in 1985 by passing a resolution calling for a Social Security COLA freeze, but this act of political daring was quashed by the White House. The "oak tree agreement" between Speaker O'Neill and Reagan, in which they mutually agreed to keep Social Security cuts and tax increases out of any deficit reduction package, resulted in few substantial savings that year.[1] Small wonder that deficit frustration was particularly strong in Senate Republican circles. They had taken a political risk, and had nothing to show for it.

One such angry lawmaker was Senator Warren Rudman (R-N.H.). On August 1, 1985, on the Senate floor he denounced the results of the budget conference: "The Senate now finds itself with a conference report which accomplishes little. How can that be?" The reasons were political: the president and the House had "agendas in which the budget deficit problem, notwithstanding their rhetoric, does not rank very high." The House was determined to protect "statutory cost-of-living adjustments" on all entitlement programs. The White House was "unwilling to consider any measure which will lead to a revenue increase," wanted to "keep as much money flowing through the defense department as possible," and avoided "exercising any leadership on cost of living adjustments." The conference report disguised its meager savings by using "overly optimistic" economic assumptions. As a result, Rudman would oppose the resolution and also an upcoming vote on "the increase in the federal debt ceiling necessary to accommodate the outrageous deficits which are coming."[2] It was not his fault, and it was a terrible situation.

Rudman was not alone in his disillusionment; it was widespread. Marvin Leath (D-Tex.) earlier in the year had decried deficit politics as the House debated its budget resolution:

> Our president says he wants to halt these deficits, but he has yet to give us a plan to halt them that can pass this Congress. Our speaker says he wants to halt these deficits, but he has yet to give us a plan to halt them that can pass this Congress. We have all told our people that we want to halt these deficits, but most of us stop there and punch up speech nos. 10, 21, 22, or 23 and start flying off into fantasyland again. No solution that can pass. Just more rhetoric—more finger pointing—more posturing.[3]

By 1985 deficits had fomented a "panic among the responsible" that included the vast majority of lawmakers.[4] Despite this, preferences were so disparate among important actors that the whole of a package would be far less than the wishes of any lawmaker who signed off on it.

Gramm-Rudman-Hollings sought to substitute for this failure a form of aggregation by threat. Agree to a substantial deficit reduction plan or face substantial across-the-board cuts in spending of the sort no rational human would make. For GRH to work its magic, though, certain conditions would have to be met. First, the threat would have to be real, because deficit reduction challenged the most entrenched of legislative concerns—program preferences and the constituency politics reinforcing them. Allocative (both micro and macro) and distributive preferences and the political forces supporting them would have to be overcome by the threat of swift and certain fiscal punishment. Second, establishing fixed deficit targets would require agreement on a stabilization course over several years. What might that course be, and would it be wise to legislate it well in advance?

GRH aimed to overcome program politics, but in fact it proved to be a triumph of program politics. As the House and Senate quarreled over the reach of the automatic cuts (known in the language of the law as "sequestration"), they made a series of determinations about which programs deserved to be spared and which did not. Many of the calculations fueling the negotiations concerned the fate of programs. House Majority Leader Tom Foley (D-Wash.) claimed that "Gramm-Rudman is about kidnapping the only child of the president's family [the defense budget] and holding it in a dark basement and sending the president its ear."[5] Other House and Senate liberals and moderates hoped it would push the chief executive into accepting tax increases. Reagan and other conservatives liked it because it avoided tax increases and guaranteed domestic cuts.[6]

GRH shared one important characteristic with the budgeting adventure of 1981. Both were based on future wishes. If a sort of politically induced visionary economics underlay the 1981 decisions, GRH rested upon a promise of future self-discipline made appealing by years of failure. Also as in 1981, a fear of stabilization problems in 1985 helped to push reforms; Congress had accepted the conventional wisdom that perpetual deficits of over $100 billion were an immediate threat to the economy. High interest rates had exacerbated the trade deficit and could promote recession soon.[7]

Events during the passage of GRH spelled problems for the future of the reform. Congress protected favored programs, and, due to constitutional problems, the institutional means for enforcing the automatic cuts was weak. Only the pressure of external political and economic forces would make the new procedures work. GRH sought to confront ideologically entrenched and constituency-based program convictions. But they would yield only to demands from back home for either tax increases or large and specific budget cuts, to strong presidential leadership toward bipartisan deficit reduction, or to the crisis of a seriously malfunctioning economy. All were absent in 1985. The economy prompted nervousness, but the recovery proceeded along, albeit at a slower pace. President Reagan continued to reject realistic bipartisanship. Constituents continued to want it both ways, opting for budget balance alongside the protection of cherished programs.[8]

All these complications did not comport with the hopes of one Senator Phil Gramm (R-Tex.), the originator of the reform. A self-styled fiscal revolutionary, Gramm had hoped to use deficit panic and GRH as a means of enshrining his economic ideology in federal policy. That ideology involved the principles of smaller government and balanced budgets. This becomes clear through a look at the law's intellectual origins and Gramm's legislative record.

THE ORIGINS OF GRAMM-RUDMAN-HOLLINGS

Gramm sought structural changes in the budget process that would force budget balance. Given the widespread legislative frustration with deficits evident in the summer of 1985, the right venue appeared in the form of an upcoming extension of the debt ceiling, a "must pass" measure.[9] Gramm had contemplated this project for years. Upon arriving in the House as a Democrat in 1979, his first legislative proposal was an amendment to a debt-ceiling extension requiring an immediate balancing of the budget. Cosponsored by James Jones and Trent Lott, it lost by two votes on the floor.[10] In 1981 he cosponsored a bill with Majority Leader Jim Wright and Minority Whip Lott, HR 1981, requiring the budget to be balanced in one year and providing for points of order on the House floor against any spending bills brought in over the target. As a long-time associate commented: "Phil had been a student of deficit reduction for several years. Cutting the size of government is his consuming goal and he has been shrewd enough to develop a plan for how to do this. The plan was on the shelf, but fortuitous political circumstances were needed to bring it off the shelf." Those circumstances arrived in August 1985.

Gramm's "plan" derived from his theoretical approach as an economist. A former professor at Texas A&M, he was fully familiar with the writings of the "public choice" school of economics. Public choice employs microeconomic assumptions to explain political behavior. Politicians are viewed as vote-maximizers; voters will prefer more government benefits if the cost of provision can be reduced. Deficit spending permits a lower immediate price for constituent benefits by deferring full payment until later. This produces more votes for incumbents, but a rising national debt. James Buchanan and Richard Wagner, two leading public choice theorists, explain the problem:

> Debt financing reduces the perceived price of publicly provided goods and services. In response, citizen-taxpayers increase their demands for such goods and services. Preferred budget levels will be higher, and these preferences will be sensed by politicians and translated into political outcomes. . . . The possibility of borrowing allows politicians to expand rates of spending without changing current levels of taxation. Empirically, the record seems clear: the increase in future taxation that public debt implies will not generate constituency pressures comparable to those generated by increases in current taxation.[11]

Consequently, "institutional halters" on the congressional "tendency to spend without taxing, and, in consequence, to spend too much" were necessary.[12]

Gramm was eager to provide some restraints. During the debate over GRH, he paraphrased the above analysis in folksy terms. "Calling in the credit cards" of the national government was the task at hand in order to stop "runaway spending."[13] A substantially smaller government would result. This was not a recent passion. In 1974 Professor Gramm listed his "current research project" in the American Economic Association's Directory of

Members as "how to get rid of government."[14] He had long believed that smaller government and balanced budgets constituted the best stabilization strategy because large government and discretionary fiscal policy destabilized the economy.

Such criticisms of deficit spending were staples of conservative economic argument long before 1985 and had enjoyed some success in fiscal battle. Buchanan and Wagner argued in their 1977 book *Democracy in Deficit* for a constitutional amendment to require a balanced budget; an amendment passed the Senate in 1982 before failing in the House. The measure became a favorite rallying cry of those who wanted to balance the budget at a lower percentage of GNP and keep it there.[15] Nor was the idea of attaching budget reform procedures to the debt-limit extension pursued by Gramm alone in the 1980s. Senators William Armstrong (R-Colo.) and Russell Long (D-La.) introduced an amendment to a debt limit increase on November 16, 1983, that gave the president the ability to rescind certain expenditures if quarterly estimates of spending exceeded the targets of the budget resolution.[16] Both Armstrong-Long and the balanced budget amendment blamed the budget process for its results; only by changing the procedures through which fiscal decisions were made could substantive policy be improved. Gramm-Rudman-Hollings shared this logic.

Gramm circulated among his partisan colleagues during the August 1985 recess with a revised version of an old idea: tack a mandatory deficit reduction plan onto the debt-ceiling bill. He recruited the disenchanted Rudman, who signed up Hollings. Gramm then presented the concept at a Senate Republican policy lunch in mid-September. Approximately twenty hard-core conservatives had threatened to vote against the debt-limit increase, but this proposal heartened them. Majority Leader Robert Dole finally agreed to back the plan when it became clear that most Republicans favored it. It was discussed and endorsed at a Republican Senate caucus and introduced on September 25.

The original amendment provided (1) declining deficit ceilings (by $36 billion a year to zero by FY 1991), (2) an accelerated budget process schedule, (3) an elaborate score-keeping mechanism requiring joint CBO-OMB economic and deficit estimates at the beginning of each fiscal year to be used to calculate the size of the necessary sequester, (4) exemption of Social Security from any sequester, and (5) provisions that half of all sequester cuts come from nondefense entitlements. This last provision would be the focus of most legislative attention and would later be changed to require that sequesters be composed of one-half defense and one-half other spending, with other safety-net programs exempted at the insistence of the House.[17]

The plan had five large implications for national institutions and fiscal politics. First, it mandated a fiscal strategy of steady reductions in the deficit, making exceptions to the policy difficult for the legislature to effect. The president was given greater discretion to suspend the timetable than was Congress. Second, the plan allowed potentially huge alterations in spending priorities; the specific "sequester targets" became the major topic of contention as the proposal evolved. Third, the president gained considerable discretionary authority over spending at the expense of Congress. The original plan placed few specific constraints upon his formulation of a sequester order through the OMB. Fourth, the CBO and OMB were to become major fiscal policy-makers through their forecasting and sequestration calculations. The CBO duty merely had been to supply analysis to Congress; OMB traditionally proposed presidential budgets and advised the president on spending matters. This was a massive new responsibility for them both. Fifth, the congressional budget process was to be recast fundamentally. New limits on committee discretion over appropriations and authorizations through tough enforcement of budget resolutions promised to redistribute spending power away from these committees and toward the Budget committees. Spending increase amendments on the floor would be effectively outlawed unless they specified commensurate spending cuts elsewhere.

Gramm offered a plan for a future fix of the problem, based on the diagnosis that the process had produced the bad results. His proposal threatened to shake up the entrenched forces of constituency politics and lawmaker ideology that perpetuated deficits by promising bad political consequences if they were not overcome. It called for members to declare an intent to rise above program concerns through an immediate vote that would demonstrate resolve to make the tough choices—sometime soon. But just as deficit spending involved a deferral of payment of full costs, one could vote for GRH and fiscal responsibility now and worry about how to pay for it later. This free vote for fiscal prudence proved seductive amid the budget frustrations of 1985.

THE POLITICS OF PASSAGE

The actual passage of GRH was a hasty and messy process. No committee ever considered it; markup in effect first occurred on the Senate floor when the amendment was submitted. This caused delay of the debt-limit increase, so the Treasury tapped into Social Security trust funds to fund the government during the fall. Eventually Congress approved several temporary debt-limit extensions until the final passage of GRH in December. Most legislators saw some possible advantage to their own program interests in GRH, and the bill promised an arguable defense of the budget process—a member could go back home and say "now we're really serious." The Senate first passed it as an amendment to the debt-limit extension by a 72–24 margin on October 10, after which the House went immediately to conference, fearing passage of the Senate version should a floor vote occur. The first conference soon broke up due to Senate recalcitrance over House amendments. The House Democrats then had to compose their own alternative. How they did this illustrates that GRH was shaped fundamentally by program politics.[18]

House Democratic conferees met and discussed whether to compose a comprehensive alternative amendment or go down to "glorious defeat." One House proposal at the first conference, advocated by Representative David Obey (D.-Wis.), involved annually refiguring deficit targets based on economic growth, a sort of "countercyclical" stabilization wrinkle. This was hardly a major issue for the House conferees, however. The crucial issue concerned exemptions from sequestration for domestic spending programs. Henry Waxman (D-Cal.) led the forces arguing for a long list of exempt programs. Conservative Budget committee member Marvin Leath of Texas supported a much shorter list of eight programs and warned that his support for any package might be conditional on the outcome of this vote. Dissent by Leath would produce many southern Democratic defections. The Leath forces ultimately prevailed by a single vote.[19] The next morning, a short list of exempt programs was sold to the Congressional Black

Caucus on the condition that the House leadership "swear in blood" that these would not be compromised in the future. That afternoon featured a meeting of all House Democrats to approve a House alternative amendment. Foley presented the package and the party united behind it. The battle lines had been drawn at the program level; redistribution had to be preserved.

Shortly afterward the House passed the Democratic alternative by a 249–180 vote, with only one Republican and two Democrats crossing party lines. Though the "concept" of GRH had proven too politically appealing for many of them to resist, House Democrats in their alternative attempted to rewrite the stabilization strategy of Gramm's proposal and to lessen its political bite. Programs had to be saved and the president's discretion over sequestration firmly contained. The need to manage the economy countercyclically and preserve redistributive domestic spending had to circumscribe sequestration efforts. If the House had its way, CBO, a trusted congressional agency, would have primary authority over calculating the cuts. Should the Constitution interfere with the law's procedures, the law itself would be voided automatically. All this minimized the political risks of bad macro policy, program cuts, and high-handed presidential authority. The Senate responded by passing 74–24 a slightly revised version of their original plan a few days later, on November 6. A second conference would have to resolve the substantial differences between the House and Senate versions.[20]

Consider the many concerns for legislators in Gramm-Rudman-Hollings: the institutional power of Congress versus the executive, the need to cut deficits while not destabilizing the economy, the question of which programs should be subject to automatic cuts and in what degree. Which would loom as most significant in the final conference? The sticking point for House conferees first and foremost involved the programs targeted for cuts. A "blood oath" had been signed to protect eight domestic social programs; this became their central charge. The select eight included Aid to Families with Dependent Children, Supplemental Security Income, child nutrition, veterans' pensions and compensation, community and migrant health care centers, the Women's Infant's and Children's feeding program, and commodity supplemental food program. As one House leadership aide put it: "We had a lot of difficult things that we had to come to terms with the Senate on, and some of them affected the core constituencies of our party in ways fundamental to their well being. Those were the items that had to be protected at all costs."

One concession by the House deleted the countercyclical targeting provisions of their plan—the original Senate targets, requiring $36 billion in reductions each year through 1991, remained in the final agreement. This signaled a triumph of conservative "balance the budget" strategy over that of Keynesian countercyclical fiscal management. The issue was not a major one at the conference. David Obey argued strenuously for inclusion of the House language; Phil Gramm in rebuttal argued that the law had no real "teeth" without firm targets. One of the Senate conferees claimed that "in the academic world, the Obey language made sense. Our concern was that we weren't going to do anything to make it easy to wiggle out of this thing. Politically, it just led to higher deficits and we weren't going to agree to it." The Senate conferees remained intransigent; a House leadership aide recalled that the Obey language was bargained away "almost invisibly."

The core battle concerned protection of programs. Phil Gramm argued that under the House plan, well over a majority of the automatic cuts would come from defense spending, an unacceptably high proportion. In return for granting exemptions desired by the House, Gramm proposed that a maximum of half of the automatic cuts in any sequester order come from defense. Foley found these terms an acceptable basis upon which to negotiate. The House conferees then simply refused to budge on exemptions, and their Senate counterparts relented. Eight poverty programs were exempted from sequestration, and cuts were limited in five health programs.[21]

The overall agreement was quickly ratified by the conferees on December 10 and moved to the Senate floor the next day. After nine hours of desultory debate and the defeat of several amendments, the Senate agreed to the plan late on December 11. Senate adoption by a 61–31 vote followed shortly thereafter. Nine Republicans voted "no" but fully half of forty-four Democrats disapproved, with eleven of twenty northern Democrats voting against. After a brief debate, the House also passed the report, 271–154. Republicans supported it 153–24 but Democrats opposed 118–

130, with northern Democrats voting no by a substantial 108 to 60 margin. Many liberals opposed it, according to Representative George Crockett (D-Mich.) "because it threatened cuts instead of tax increases. We weren't interested in seeing domestic government shrink."

WHAT HAD THEY WROUGHT?

Senator Robert Packwood, chair of the Finance committee, spoke for many of his colleagues during final debate on the conference report when he confessed that "I am tired of economic theories."[22] Deficit reduction was to be achieved, by whatever means necessary, voluntary or mandatory. Let the chips then fall where they may. Congress, as in 1981, had improvised with fiscal theory in pursuit of a solution to political vexations. Democrats found themselves formally repudiating Keynes again in order to "get serious about the deficit," for the plan clearly derived from conservative economic thought. The government could only stabilize the economy for growth by moving to budget balance and staying there. The sacrifice of fiscal discretion was fixed in law, however, and not in the constitution, as the most ardent conservatives had wished. And that law was under constitutional challenge within days of its signing by the president.

Its passage is a testament to Phil Gramm's tactical prowess and the tenacity of House Democrats in protecting their favored programs. The final version as a result is oddly conservative in its fiscal theory and liberal in its program protections. It was a congressionally generated product whose politics primarily were internal. Within Congress, the process was a "collegial" chamber-dominated affair with party leaders and bill sponsors serving as brokers, extraordinary in its intensity due to the "must pass" debt-limit extension and seeming urgency of the deficit problem.[23] So many cooks produced an extremely rich broth.

The underlying assumption among many supporters of the bill remained that the deficits resulted from a flawed budget process and that only through procedural reform could the federal budget be balanced. Actually, congressional political economy dictated an unsuccessful process. The fault lay in the constituency-ideology program nexus of lawmakers that prevented the institution from approving annual budget plans consistent with long-term deficit reduction. And an empirically correct rationalization—"it's not my fault"—was available to all legislators who sought to alleviate personal stress over deficit politics while demanding protection for programs. Congressional leaders thus had to press for program rigidities in the formula; the president added similar constraints. Senator Mark Hatfield (R-Ore.) at the time accurately put the problem: "Our current predicament lies not so much with the present congressional budget process as with our will to make it work, and no new system, no matter how cleverly contrived, will work unless we summon the will and courage to make it work."[24] The process was not the source of the problem, merely its location.

The "process" indictment betrays a fundamental misreading of deficits. Revised internal procedures, particularly those with a questionable constitutional future, would not deliver a solution. Congressional action to tackle the deficits had to be driven by forces outside the institution. Demands for action from the elite opinion leaders of the political stratum could produce pressure on legislators, but could not overcome the bastion of personal and constituency beliefs in programs. All the political stratum could do was increase stress and compel a rush to rationalization. Other forces had more impact. Strong and unambiguous demands for change from a president popular with constituents propelled the 1981 budget revolution. Economic reversal in the form of a stock market crash would spawn a budget summit in 1987—a sinking economy alongside huge deficits could drown a presidency along with lawmakers' constituents and favorite programs. But no such forces operated in 1985. Without a push from them, Congress would not act.

The legislature invented new procedures in order to force choices, and, as in 1981, the political theory underlying a sweeping fiscal reform was flawed—the political preconditions for deficit reduction simply did not exist in 1985. Ironically, time spent on Gramm-Rudman-Hollings prevented passage of reconciliation legislation for FY 1986 (which began October 1) by the time Congress adjourned in December. The immediate problem had only grown worse by year's end. To counter the deteriorating situation, GRH assumed that preferences and incentives would change with the new threat of automatic cuts. This all depended upon the effectiveness of the new mechanism. Would threats of hammerblows be sufficient to forge a consensus? Given a growing economy and public ambivalence about the deficit, the entrenched program concerns of legislators provided a strong motive to find ways to avoid the blows without wrenching fiscal changes. A powerful incentive for lying about fiscal policy now operated. That is the story of the remainder of the decade.

GRH IN PRACTICE

Budget scholars have identified accurately other flawed features of GRH. Allen Schick notes that it lacked adequate mechanisms to control spending for two reasons. First, the size of the cuts depended upon economic projections, encouraging fanciful projections—a problem particularly evident after the GRH "fix" in 1987, when power for forecasts was entrusted with OMB. Second, "after October 15, additional spending cannot trigger the GRH process, no matter what it does to the deficit."[25] In addition, the notion that "budget policy should look inward to correcting its own imbalances rather than the country's is not fully implementable."[26] Revenues and outlays are altered by economic conditions, and legislators cannot be expected to ignore the environment outside of Congress and simply focus on budget totals. This, in addition to the lack of enforcement of targets once the fiscal year began, meant that the law's targets were easily violated, as they were for all of the remaining fiscal years of the decade.

White and Wildavsky note that an ironic consequence of the law was an increase in incentives not for speedier budgeting, but for delay: "All the incentives in GRH worked to make delay strategically advisable; too much was taken off the table; the reason the act was passed in the first place—inability to agree on the budget—caused participants to seek their own solutions rather than compromise; and, at the last moment, the only option was to obfuscate."[27] All this meant that the law would not substantially transform the political economy of legislators. Established ways of thinking and acting would overcome the law's "parchment barriers."

GRH did highlight fiscal contradictions when Congress annually rushed to comply with its targets on paper while maintaining much budgeting as usual. It could only be effective by shaming lawmakers into compliance. But when defending low taxes or spending programs, most legislators felt no shame. They were true to their convictions and supporting electoral coalitions, and fault lay elsewhere. Budgeting as usual would yield only after an emphatic and politically costly show of presidential intransigence by George Bush in 1990.

GRH certainly did not lessen Washington's fixation on fiscal issues. In 1986 alone, in addition to arduous work on the budget, Congress restructured comprehensively the federal tax system, the Senate defeated narrowly a constitutional amendment mandating a balanced budget, and the federal courts complicated matters by voiding a key enforcement provision of the Gramm-Rudman-Hollings process. The court action confused fiscal politics and made remote the likelihood that meaningful cuts would be enforced through the sequester process.

A three-judge panel of the Federal District Court of the District of Columbia on February 7 held that the role of the General Accounting Office (GAO) in the GRH process was unconstitutional. The GAO's duty in the law was to finally formulate and promulgate sequesters. The agency, with a long-standing reputation for integrity, would decide on economic assumptions when calculating the size of a sequester. GAO was not likely to use funny numbers to lessen cuts. The court ruled that the powers entrusted to the Comptroller General, head of the GAO, were executive powers, which could not constitutionally be exercised by an officer removable by Congress. The Supreme Court agreed by a 7–2 margin on July 7. This meant the "fall back" provision of the law would now have to be implemented if any cuts were to occur. That required a joint committee to approve a sequester order and both chambers to pass it. Fat chance.[28] Representative Leon Panetta (D-Calif.) at the time noted to colleagues that the law provided no specific penalty for failure of the joint committee or either chamber to approve a sequester order.[29]

Instead, Congress in 1987 "fixed" GRH by setting easy targets and allowing OMB to cook the numbers, ensuring an evasion of discipline. Faced with the politically impossible task of meeting the mandated $108 billion deficit level, Congress revised upward the targets so that substantial deficit reduction would have to wait for a new president and Congress in 1989. A deficit-cutting package did pass in December 1987, largely as a result of an astounding one-day drop in the stock market two months before. But the measure at best met the revised GRH targets that required only minor shrinkage of the deficit until after the 1988 elections. Then, supposedly, the problem would be solved through the necessary tough choices.

In the meantime, the red ink flowed at levels well over $100 billion annually and the deficit panic of the political stratum continued. But still the sky did not fall; this justification of one's deficit voting could be more plausibly argued with each passing year. Congress could avoid the rigors of GRH by making targets easier and inflating the scale of deficit reduction efforts with deceitful tricks.[30] With a growing economy and no clear policy direction evident in public opinion, programs retained their place at the center of legislative life. A brief summary of the politics and results of the years 1986–89 so indicates.

1986: TAX MANNA AND A SUPPORTIVE ECONOMY

After lengthy negotiations that overshot the new budget timetable by months, Congress agreed on a reconciliation package less than three weeks before the mid-term elections. It totaled a mere $11.7 billion, more than $8 billion of which were "gimmicks"—asset sales and other one-time savings—and $3.7 billion in additional revenues originally proposed by the administration. Social Security costs actually grew as a result of the agreement because the three percent inflation "trigger" for COLAs was abolished.[31] Pete Domenici labeled the agreement "not even close to a good solution." Marvin Leath termed it "the ultimate scam."[32] The large margins of victory for the package on the House and Senate floors resulted from its small-scale and politically inoffensive content.

Delays in budget negotiations forced the House Appropriations committee to wrap all thirteen appropriations bills into an omnibus continuing resolution for the first time since 1950. As the fiscal year began, the chambers wrestled with passage of the largest appropriations bill in the history of the republic, a $576 billion continuing resolution. The "must pass" measure became a magnet for all manner of program spending concerns and other issues of the moment. Its conference in early October was protracted by numerous amendments; the White House threatened a veto. Final passage did not come until October 17.

Congress was saved in this instance by an economy that grew at rates higher than predicted earlier in the year, thus reducing the size of the deficit, and also by consequences of the sweeping 1986 tax reform. Short-term oscillations in revenue flows resulting from the tax bill would produce an $11 billion windfall for FY 1987 that insured compliance with the GRH target. The final numbers showed a deficit just a whisker under $150 billion, within the $10 billion margin of error allowed by the law for hitting the $144 billion target. Legislators still found reasons to argue the program contents of a package among themselves and with the White House, since this was the first year of GRH and it was time, according to budget captains, to get serious by using a sound economy as a rationale for larger cuts.

But the events of 1986 proved that GRH had not forced a new fiscal consensus upon Congress. Further evidence of this in the attitudes of individual lawmakers is displayed in table 5–1. A survey of House and Senate offices in May allowed identification of GRH opponents and supporters.[33] The questionnaire included two items on GRH: (1) The Gramm-Rudman-Hollings act promotes responsible deficit reduction. (2) The Gramm-Rudman-Hollings act should be repealed. Opinion on these items divided sharply along partisan lines. At one pole stood Republicans in both chambers—57 percent of them in the House and 63 percent in the Senate opposed repeal; 50 percent in the House and 63 percent in the Senate approved of its effects. Northern Democrats, at the other extreme, approved repeal in greater proportions—56 percent in the House and 40 percent in the Senate—while 28 percent in the House and 48 percent in the Senate thought the law promoted responsible deficit reduction. Southern Democrats occupied a middle ground. In the House 44 percent thought GRH promoted sound deficit policy and 38 percent wanted repeal; in the Senate the proportions were 63 percent and only 13 percent. The Senate, where the law originated, opposed repeal and approved of its consequences more than did the House. Of Senators, 63 percent approved of GRH and opposed repeal; in the House

TABLE 5–1   Characteristics of Congressional Gramm-Rudman-Hollings Supporters and Neutrals/Opponents in 1986[1]

		House (N = 253)		Senate (N = 67)	
		%D	%R	%D	%R
Party	Pro GRH	29	66**	45	69*
	Other	71	34	55	31
		%Y	%N	%Y	%N
Balance budget	Pro GRH	64	15**	71	44*
every year	Other	36	85	29	56
Reduce inequality	Pro GRH	29	62**	41	67**
	Other	71	38	59	33
Freeze defense	Pro GRH	60	40**	36	75**
	Other	40	60	64	25
Increase revenues	Pro GRH	28	68**	48	88*
	Other	72	32	52	12

		Good	Uncert.	Bad	Good	Uncert.	Bad
National econ.	Pro GRH	55	34	0**	67	48	—
expectations (1 year)	Other	45	66	100	33	52	—
National econ.	Pro GRH	66	59	19**	81	53	38*
expectations (long-term)	Other	34	41	81	19	47	63

		Mean[2]			Mean[2]		
ADA score	Pro GRH	29.9**			35.2**		
	Other	59.1			63.2		
Presidential sup-	Pro GRH	56.2**			62.5**		
port score	Other	37.2			45.7		

*Differences significant at .05 level
**Differences significant at .01 level.
[1]All percentages are column percentages. Not all tabulations included the total number of responses due to failure of some respondents to complete the item.
[2]Significance established by a t-test of paired means.

overall 50 percent approved of its effects and 60 percent opposed repeal.

To discern congressional reception to GRH in practice, respondents were divided into supporters of GRH (those favoring its effects and opposing repeal) and a category of neutrals and opponents (all other respondents). The law first needed strong majority support to have a chance of success; it did not have it in 1986. GRH supporters constituted a mere 46 percent of House members and 54 percent of Senators.[34] If these findings were representative of congressional opinion, one could hypothesize that the legislature would disregard the law's rigor in the pursuit of more closely held fiscal values. In fact, that is what happened after 1985. The fiscal status quo would not be budged by GRH alone.

A widespread consensus on the law would also require that members with varying ideologies, party affiliations, and fiscal opinions support it. Table 5–1 indicates that this was not the case. In both chambers, Republicans favored GRH more than Democrats, presidential supporters more than opponents, conservatives more than liberals.[35] GRH supporters possessed a distinctly conservative ideology, being significantly more likely than opponents to support annual budget balance and oppose governmental redistribution, freezing defense, and raising revenues. They also had more optimistic expectations for the economy during the next year and the long-term.

TABLE 5–2   Influences upon the Senate
Vote on the FY 1987 Budget Resolution[1]

Percentage saying very influential	Pro-GRH	Other
Personal convictions	92	85
Constituents	57	48*
Party leaders	32	12
GRH act	58	12**
Staff	22	44
Budget comm. chair or ranking member	27	35
Budget comm. members	9	4
Other colleagues	6	8
President	14	—**
Lobbyists	—	—

*Difference between the groups significant at the .05 level.
**Difference between the groups significant at the .01 level.
[1]Overall N = 67. The total number of responses to each of the above items did not always equal 67 as some items were not completed by respondents. Significance tests were conducted for the items by GRH support/opposition.

TABLE 5–3   Influences upon the House
Vote on the FY 1987 Budget Resolution[1]

Percentage saying very influential	Pro-GRH	Other
Personal convictions	94	91
Constituents	61	56
Party leaders	41	37
GRH act	59	24**
Staff	28	26
Budget comm. chair or ranking member	18	27
Budget comm. members	8	10
Other colleagues	6	5
President	27	7**
Lobbyists	—	4

** Difference between the groups significant at the .01 level.
[1] Overall N = 253. The total number of responses to each of the above items did not always equal 253 as some items were not completed by respondents. Significance tests were conducted for the items by GRH support/opposition.

Further evidence of the political distinctiveness of the law's supporters is found in Tables 5–2 and 5–3. In budget resolution voting, both the president and GRH law influenced GRH supporters much more than other legislators. Overall, GRH was approved by primarily the ideologically conservative; it had many enemies and would not command the allegiance it needed now that effective sequestration had been voided by the courts. Procedural rigor would not be restored by any GRH "fix" devised by a legislature so divided on the merits of the law itself, particularly once the Democrats won back the Senate in the autumn of 1986.

1987: UNLOADING THE GUN

The advent of a Democratic Senate for the first time in six years also did not augur well for fiscal compromise. In addition to the consequent partisan standoff between president and Congress, realistic economic forecasts made attainment of the $108 billion target in 1987 politically impossible. This invited legislative "improvement" of the GRH framework. Republicans fought for generous deficit targets for 1988 and 1989 to prevent embarrassment to the administration; Democrats wanted targets tough enough to force concessions on taxes. The threat of a veto allowed Republican forces to prevail. The agreement limited the total amount of deficit reduction necessary in FY 1988 to $23 billion and in FY 1989 to $36 billion. But tinkering with the baseline for calculating cuts made this discipline far less than it seemed. The innovation of an inflation-adjusted baseline automatically assumed another $13 billion in spending, resulting in an estimate that the $23 billion cut would only yield about $10 billion in actual savings.[36]

Despite the small amount necessary to avoid sequester, Congress and the president remained at loggerheads over how to raise it. Reagan steadfastly opposed any tax increases. The plan of the Democratic Congress called for $19.3 billion in additional revenues. The resultant stalemate squelched progress on appropriations and reconciliation; by October 1 not one spending bill had passed Congress. The outlook was quite bleak until economic events intervened on October 19, causing legislators to revise drastically their theories about the economy.

As a result of an unprecedented 22.6 percent drop in the value of the Dow Jones industrial average on that day—508 points—and large dips in other stock markets around the world, the need to stem "market turmoil" loosened presidential rigidity on taxes and produced a deficit reduction package that just avoided imposition of sequester. It is difficult to argue a causation between deficit politics and a market plummet; after all, deficits had been around all decade, so why would they force a fall now?[37] Nevertheless, the political stratum—economists and media institutions, both nationally and internationally—focused upon the American deficit as a probable cause. Panic was again in the air; now it seemed the sky might just fall after all.

Though the American and international stock markets encountered weeks of nervousness after October 19, a further big drop did not occur. And unlike 1981, no public demand for particular stabilization tactics emerged. The panic was an elite, not a popular, phenomenon. Senator Robert Packwood, a budget summit participant, recalled: "When the stock market crashed was there an outcry from our constituents? No."[38] Public sentiment pointed in no sensible fiscal direction; a CBS News/*New York Times* poll in November showed the public demanding budget balance but opposing higher taxes, Social Security cuts, and substantially lower defense spending. Fiscal contradictions in public opinion had been evident since 1982 and had made any plausible deficit solution politically risky.[39] Legislators had long realized that it was easy to offend voters about parts of the budget while pursuing resolute action concerning the whole.

The receding sense of urgency boosted the importance of program-level concerns in the negotiations; lessening macroeconomic problems could not force an immediate consensus. The negotiations themselves were a bizarre example of tactical governance based on daily economic events. Senator Rudy Boschwitz (R-Minn.), pressing for action, was informed by White House chief of staff Howard Baker and Pete Domenici that "everybody in the room is watching the market and if the market is good today, there is no need to agree. What we need is another market bust to force the issue." The conferees in December finally settled upon a two-year accord providing the minimum necessary to avoid sequestration, $25.2 billion in reductions for FY 1988 and $42 billion for FY 1989. Among the contents of the FY 1988 package were $5 billion from defense, $9 billion in taxes, and $4 billion in entitlement reforms (mainly in Medicare). The agreement effectively settled the major "macro" allocation (size of government) and economic stabilization issues of fiscal policy for the remainder of the Reagan presidency. Deficit targets were set and the parameters of spending fixed.

By the time Congress adjourned at 4:26 A.M. on December 22, 1987, the necessary fiscal legislation was finally in place. For the second consecutive year, a series of temporary continuing resolutions had given the legislature time to do its work. Gaining approval were a reconciliation bill claiming to reduce the deficit by $76 billion over two years and an omnibus appropriations bill in the record-total amount of $609 billion in budget authority to fund the government for the remainder of FY 1988. End-of-session squabbles involved the traditional topics of budgeting—program spending in its allocative and distributive aspects. Constrained by the budget limits of the summit, negotiations between Senate, House, and White House over the particulars of spending became lengthy and draining.[40] Events forced all issues into the budget process at the same time; only the lure of the holidays prompted summary judgments by late in the month.

1988: THE YEAR OF THE BIG WINK

The year 1988 proved to be the calmest fiscal year of the decade because Congress quietly resurrected several dubious budget tactics in order to keep money flowing to favored programs. Funny economic assumptions and questionable spending classifications made 1988 a giant evasion of the fiscal problem and earned it a nickname on the Hill as the "year of the big wink." The summit agreement approved in 1987 had provided spending limits for major areas of the budget for both FY 1988 and FY 1989—defense, entitlements, international affairs, and domestic discretionary spending. The administration budget proposal claimed to stay within the guidelines, but Congress had its own programmatic battles to fight within the caps and did not adhere to the White House plan. The legislature in 1988 merely had to approve a budget resolution and spending bills staying within the legal limits; no reconciliation bill was necessary. Persistent if modest economic growth facilitated deferral of the problem, though the economy would not perform well enough to validate the deliberately wishful thinking of congressional budgeteers.

The House and Senate overwhelmingly passed resolutions that seemed to affirm the summit agreement, but each chamber displayed dubious creativity in the particulars of its work. Both chambers accepted OMB economic assumptions in order to hit the revised GRH target of $136 billion; in fact the deficit for that year would overshoot the target and its $10 billion fudge factor and stand at $155 billion. The House found ways to "reclassify" some spending in the summit agreement from discretionary to mandatory in order to free up money for discretionary domestic programs like education and job training. The Senate appended monies for space programs and antidrug efforts that seemingly violated the caps. When it came time to work out domestic program claims in conference, proceedings turned nasty. After weeks of negotiation, a compromise resolution gave each chamber a little of what it wanted but curtailed some of the reclassification by the

House. The spending battles then shifted to the Appropriations committees, which had to allocate monies within the caps. In the end, Congress exceeded both the GRH target (by $25 billion) and the discretionary spending target of the 1987 summit (by $2 billion), but the White House chose to look the other way as elections impended.[41]

1989: ANOTHER PRESIDENT, ANOTHER WINK

The election of George Bush on a fiscal platform identical to that of Reagan, alongside increased numbers of Democrats in the House and Senate, hardly improved chances of compromise. The Bush budget proposal contained a raft of budget gimmicks necessary to meet the $100 billion GRH target with a minimum of difficult choices. Subterfuges included optimistic economic assumptions, creative accounting on a number of programs, and a refusal to identify specific domestic cuts necessary to hit the target. Further, the $17 billion in revenues in the Bush plan included $4.8 billion in first-year savings from a capital gains tax cut. This proposal violated distributional convictions among moderate and liberal Democrats and would produce pitched battles between the Democratic leadership in Congress and the president, further complicating budget politics.

In April the White House and Congress supposedly solved that year's fiscal problem with a budget summit agreement entailing $28 billion in savings. But at the time, parties to the plan concurred that it was gimmick-ridden. Resolutions embodying the agreement passed the House and Senate, but the revenue committee balked at raising $5.3 billion required by the agreement. At this point the administration tried some brinkmanship with capital gains, demanding it be included in the budget package. Democratic resistance produced a long delay and temporary imposition of a sequester. But the cuts had lost their power to intimidate. When asked whether he feared a sequester, House Majority Whip William Gray (D-Pa.) responded: "Absolutely not. Because every year we know that, one, there will be something worked out that avoids it and, number two, every two or three years Republicans will modify the targets to make them easier to reach."[42] A battle-weary Pete Domenici claimed that "the planned train wreck is not being taken as seriously as it was originally. There are a lot of gimmicks around and people have learned to use them, so that a major sequestration hasn't happened."[43]

Bush was forced to relent and demanded $14.7 billion in real deficit reduction in return for dropping capital gains. A reconciliation bill in this amount finally passed on November 22. Though the bill was for the first time in the decade stripped of extraneous proposals tacked on by lawmakers to further program interests, it nevertheless contained at least $2.9 billion in bookkeeping shell games.[44] The uniform consensus held that the GRH target would be exceeded again.

1990: A BIG DEAL

The 1990 deficit actually totaled $220 billion, double the $110 billion GRH target supposedly aimed for in 1989. Despite or perhaps because of this failure, 1990 witnessed adoption of sweeping deficit reduction and budget process changes. In October, a five-year $496 billion package of "real" deficit reductions gained approval, as did a reform of the budget process that set actual statutory caps for spending in domestic, international, and defense program areas.[45] The measure promised to restrain the deficit substantially and still allow Congress to continue to appropriate as usual within the new limits. The painful action necessary to begin movement toward a new fiscal era finally occurred in 1990, with its prime instigator—George Bush—incurring most of the political damage.

The year 1990 initially promised to be a dispiriting repeat of the fakery of preceding budget rounds. The administration presented a proposal that met the $64 billion GRH target for FY 1991 with many rosy economic assumptions. It included a priority mix that congressional Democrats derided as unfair and unrealistic— only a two percent real cut in defense, cancellation of twenty-four domestic programs, a capital gains tax cut, and few substantial increases in revenues. With the cold war rapidly waning, Democrats in both chambers sought much deeper defense cuts and more domestic social spending. Neither side would be the first to advocate the substantial additional taxes necessary for a long-term deficit solution. The House on May 1 passed a budget resolution providing for deep cuts in defense and fanciful economic assumptions.[46] All this suggested yet another partisan standoff on issues of allocation and distribution.

By early May, new budget projections suggested that a sequester would amount to more than $100 billion unless the impasse was resolved. The White House agreed to begin what was to be a lengthy budget summit with a bipartisan group of congressional leaders with "no preconditions." For Democrats, that meant possible entitlement cuts were on the table, including that potential political powder keg, Social Security. For Republicans and the White House, possible tax increases had to be countenanced. This was the first, and least, of what was to become a series of political costly deviations by George Bush from his famous 1988 campaign declaration: "Read my lips—no new taxes!"

For almost two months, the meetings produced little progress as the administration and congressional Republicans stuck with their demand for domestic spending cuts and resistance to taxes while Democrats clung to their domestic priorities and demanded the president "go first" in publicly endorsing tax increases. On June 26 Bush broke the standoff by announcing at a press conference that "tax revenue increases" had to be part of a deficit reduction plan.[47] But this merely permitted the talks to continue and did not push them closer to a final compromise. Republicans would not first commit to tax increases, and Democrats would not first commit to entitlement cuts. The economy had begun to slow, making the $64 billion GRH target for FY 1991 even more elusive. Congressional frustration with the standoff was growing. On July 17 a constitutional amendment for a balanced budget failed in the House by a mere seven votes, the closest margin ever.[48] Many lawmakers shared the summiteers' belief that large and growing deficits had to be stemmed, but program concerns remained ever-present in Congress. One day later, the House Republican conference approved by a 2–1 margin a resolution opposing any tax increases—their long-held allocation views would die hard, if they died at all. Appropriators in both chambers meanwhile had begun their work without the passage of a final budget resolution.

Summit discussions nevertheless proceeded, for the negotiators agreed that if a package could be produced with $50 billion in deficit reductions in 1991 and $500 billion over five years, sequestration could be avoided. The president remained firm that sequestration would occur if such a deal was not struck. Unlike his predecessor, Bush now would put overall deficit reduction ahead of many specific programmatic goals. Democratic and Republican congressional negotiators took seriously their obligation to govern responsibly by addressing the deficit. By mid-September, only one month from the sequestration deadline, it became clear that the administration's proposal for a capital gains tax cut remained a major stumbling block.[49] Democratic negotiators framed their position in distributive terms, arguing that the cut benefited the wealthy. Senate Majority Leader George Mitchell (D-Me.) claimed that "you can't have a tax package that says one group will be exempt from sacrifice, and especially if that group is the most fortunate and well-off among Americans."[50] This theme would constitute a politically advantageous refrain for Democrats in the coming weeks.

The talks wore on until the eve of the fiscal year, when negotiators agreed upon a package, in the form of a budget reconciliation bill, totalling $500 billion in deficit reductions over five years. Bush had been forced to abandon a capital gains tax cut, and Democrats managed to avoid any cuts in Social Security. But the package contained something to offend programmatic preferences and constituency of just about every legislator. New taxes and user fees summing to $147.7 billion over five years outraged conservative Republicans in the House. Plans to increase payments by Medicare recipients some $27.8 billion offended many Democrats, as did the fact that the tax hike for the poor in the package was much higher proportionately than for those making over $200,000 a year.[51] Few were keen to increase the gas tax 10 cents per gallon in the midst of a Persian Gulf crisis. Higher taxes on alcohol and tobacco were not popular with many legislators, and rural lawmakers could object to the $13 billion reduction in farm price-support payments.[52]

The response was sharply negative in the House, where each party established battle lines of economic ideology for the fight over the package. Most House Republicans would denounce it on grounds of macroallocation; it raised taxes and kept spending at too high a level. The president and minority leader lobbied their members, but the minority whip, Newt Gingrich of Georgia, opposed the plan, thus depriving them of the party whip organization for their efforts. Many House Democrats seized upon distributive fairness in their criticism of the package. Speaker Foley and the Democratic leadership were forced to backpedal from endorsement of the plan's specifics when confronted with a harshly critical Democratic caucus. Though Foley spoke of the plan as only a general blueprint that could be altered by subsequent House action, his comments did not convince many Democrats, but instead made Republicans even more nervous about Democratic schemes to alter the package if initially adopted.

Both the White House and Democratic leadership aimed to get a majority of their fellow partisans to support the plan, but it lost overwhelmingly on the House floor, 179–254, in the early morning of October 5. The ideological argument was predictable. Democrat Bob Wise (W.Va.) claimed the package allowed the rich "to make out like bandits, while my people get hit again." Republican Dick Armey (Tex.) argued that he preferred sequestration because it "hurts government, and this package hurts the American people and their economy" by raising taxes.[53] The president immediately warned that sequestration was in the offing. He had signed a continuing resolution and debt-limit extension to fund government through October 5. On October 6 he vetoed another continuing resolution, causing the government to shut down all nonessential services. Tourists in the capital for the Columbus day weekend found the Washington Monument and Smithsonian closed. Congress then rapidly passed a budget resolution affirming the aggregate parameters of the summit plan. It also approved another continuing resolution, which the president this time signed on October 9.

What followed next were ten days of partisan maneuvering and confusion over what the president's preferences on taxation actually were. Bush publicly vacillated on whether capital gains should be in or out of the package, and on whether he would accept an extension of the top marginal individual tax rate to 33 percent in return for this. Senate Republicans told him not to budge on the top rate; House Republicans tried to interest him in a plan to raise the top rate slightly in return for a generous capital gains cut. Senate Democrats, led by Senator Lloyd Bentsen, tried to negotiate a bipartisan plan in their chamber, with one ear to what the White House wanted. Both Majority Leader Mitchell and Minority Leader Dole found substantial support among their members for a bipartisan approach. Bentsen was forced to proceed toward bipartisan consensus in committee due to its one-seat Democratic majority and the reluctance of member Bill Bradley (D-N.J.) and committee Republicans to go along with a key Democratic demand to raise the top income tax rate.

House Democrats meanwhile went their own way, fashioning a reconciliation bill with much more progressive tax increases and fewer entitlement cuts.[54] Their relish was abundant at having again found political initiative in distribution issues. Democrats pasted Bush's indecision as an example of Republicans trying to protect the rich from paying more taxes. On October 16 the Democratic alternative passed the House, 238–192. A representative expression of Democratic glee during the debate came from House member Larry Smith (D-Fla.), who challenged Republicans: "Whether you like it or not, whether the president likes it or not, we are going to have a progressive tax policy that works for America."[55] Republicans charged the "tax-a-crats" with big taxing and spending plans, and some voiced fear that tax increases would hurt the economy on the brink of recession. But stabilization remained quite a minor theme in the politics of October.[56] Once the president had set firmly the parameters for a long-term deal, congressional battle lines concerned specific taxing and spending policies—just as in the passage of GRH five years earlier. Distributive fairness provided strong partisan momentum for House Democrats.

This momentum did not stretch to the Senate, however, which passed a bipartisan resolution by a 54–46 margin on October 19 after defeating Republican amendments to cut taxes and Democratic efforts to enhance tax progressivity. Party leaders Mitchell and Dole fought hard against efforts to dismantle the reconciliation bill produced by Bentsen's Finance committee in order to pass a package the White House might find agreeable as a basis for bargaining. The House and Senate plans differed substantially on both taxes and spending cuts, resulting in a conference in which the White House actively participated.[57] The president agreed to continuing resolutions to let negotiations proceed until final agreement came on October 27, when the House and Senate narrowly passed the package by margins of 228–200 and 54–45, respectively. The proximity of the elections—less than two weeks away—

finally wore down resistance. Democrats found the plan more acceptable, providing support from a majority of their members in both chambers. Though the Senate produced a substantial fraction of Republicans (19 of 45) in support, in the House only 47 of 173 Republicans voted yes.

The political costs of the victory were substantial for George Bush. His public popularity as measured in opinion polls, fell substantially during the chaotic October.[58] The long-standing and politically valuable Republican argument against higher taxes had been traded for supposed deficit reduction, resulting in strong resentment among Republican conservatives in Congress. The staff director of the Republican Congressional Campaign Committee urged his candidates to run against any new taxes during the election campaign, prompting a White House suggestion that he should be fired. Capital gains tax reductions remained only a partisan wish. Democrats stood ready to bash the GOP on the fairness issue in any future budget tangle. As Representative Bill Frenzel (R-Minn.) stated: "They beat us to death with this rich and poor thing."[59]

THE CONSEQUENCES OF 1990

The theatrics of October initially served to obscure the significance of many of the features of the deficit reduction package. Its important provisions fall into three categories: the programmatic content of the package, its budget process changes, its effect on future budget deficits. Democrats and liberals could claim victory on much of the program content of the package, but the White House and conservatives gained important restraints on spending in the budget process that would remain in effect through the first half of the 1990s. The package also promised unprecedented real deficit reductions that would lessen the red ink substantially.

The final package contained $496 billion in deficit reduction over five years and a number of provisions that made it much more acceptable to liberal Democrats than the initial summit package. The top income tax rate rose from 28 percent to 31 percent for the highest income taxpayers, raising some $11.2 billion over five years.[60] A regressive gas tax was scaled back to five cents per gallon from the higher levels of the initial package and Senate plan;

a tax on fuel oil was eliminated. Increases in Medicare payments were reduced dramatically from earlier plans, and the wage cap for Medicare payroll taxes increased substantially, from $51,300 to $125,000. The defense spending reduction, while a bipartisan compromise at $182 billion over five years, was far greater than the administration had initially countenanced. Overall, the final plan was more progressive in its imposition of taxes than the first summit plan or that proposed by the Senate in mid-October. Those making over $200,000 annually would pay 6.3 percent more in taxes, close to the 7.4 percent in plan that passed the House on October 16.[61]

Immediate press attention focused on what seemed to be a Democratic triumph over the White House on the above items, but failed to note adequately the sweeping changes in the budget process also included in the reconciliation bill. Here, George Bush eagerly claimed victory: "The tough enforcement provisions are tougher than I ever thought we could get in any way from this Congress."[62] Two particular mechanisms—spending caps and a pay-as-you-go requirement for new programs—promised to make major changes in specific spending decisions more difficult. The caps set specific legal limits, adjusted annually for inflation, for FY 1991–1993 in each of three discretionary spending areas: defense international aid, and domestic spending.[63] The caps derived from the totals in the deficit reduction agreement. Pay-as-you-go required all new spending legislation to be revenue neutral from FY 1991–1995, meaning it had to include other spending cuts or tax increases to pay for new programs. This would hamstring efforts by authorizing committees to advance new spending programs.

Each of these provisions would be enforced by sequesters, and compliance with each restraint would be calculated solely by the Office of Management and Budget. If OMB found spending to have exceeded a cap, an across-the-board cut could be declared in that spending area, to take effect fifteen days after Congress adjourned. A violation of pay-as-you-go would result in similar cuts affecting entitlements not exempt from sequestration. GRH-style aggregate sequestrations were dropped for 1991–93, and could be dropped at presidential option for 1994–95.[64]

All this promised strict controls on spending to be enforced by OMB. In effect, the caps made budget resolutions insignificant, and transferred power over fiscal decisions to the Appropriations committees, which would make specific decisions within the caps. Pay-as-you-go promised to sharply limit the ability of authorizing committees to propose new spending plans. The composite effect promised to return budgeting to its Appropriations-centered pattern of before the 1974 Budget act.

And that was exactly what Jamie Whitten and Robert Byrd, chairs of the Appropriations committees, desired. It was Byrd who took the initiative during the summit negotiations in pressing for agreement on these procedures with the White House. The chairs of the Budget and authorizing committees were otherwise occupied and let the issue go. In addition to restricting the powers of the meddlesome Budget committees, Byrd obtained a domestic spending cap of $38 billion above inflation for FY 1991–1993. But since authorizing committees would be hampered by pay-as-you-go, Appropriations would be the place for the money to be spent. OMB and the Appropriations committees would be the centers of budgeting, just like in the old days.[65] If the framework stayed in place, firm spending control would become a reality for the first time in at least a decade.

Stabilization had not been a major theme of battle in 1990; most agreed that some form of deficit reduction was appropriate even though recession seemed imminent. Keynes was not resurrected for the debate. However, the new law provided that spending above the overall FY 1991–93 budget targets could be ordered due to macroeconomic changes, such as a downturn that boosted automatic spending—a concession to "common sense" countercyclical policy long endorsed by most lawmakers. The plan at minimum kept the deficit from getting worse than it actually did due to recession. It may prove to reduce the deficit significantly by mid-decade. Though FY 1991 at the time of this writing threatened a $298 billion deficit, many observers—including the CBO— expected that with moderate economic growth, the deficit would fall below $170 billion by 1995.[66] This constitutes a level near three percent of GNP despite the fact that Social Security with its large surplus (over $58 billion in 1990 and destined to rise to $114 billion by 1995) for the first time has been moved off-budget.[67] This would be real progress. But can the program aspirations of

Congress be held in check long enough for this good news to arrive?

CONCLUSION

Though fiscal responsibility appeared suddenly in 1990, its persistence on the national stage is uncertain. Its prospects seem tenuous once we grasp why it seemed to prevail in 1990. This did not occur due to the "teeth" of Gramm-Rudman-Hollings, but rather because of the resolve of George Bush to stop "spending as usual" unless long-term deficit reduction became law. As the late 1980s abundantly demonstrated, sequestration could be readily avoided, should the president and Congress desire to do so. Presidential resolve to consummate a deal and flexibility on program specifics ultimately produced long-term deficit reduction, not GRH. George Bush demonstrated his seriousness in 1990 more by vetoing a continuing resolution than by threatening a sequester. The "stick" of GRH, while helpful, was not essential to the outcome of the 1990 budget battle. The final reconciliation bill reflects this in its replacement of the GRH mechanism for sweeping budget cuts with more finely-tuned and stringent enforcement machinery.

GRH may have kept the deficit from getting worse than it did in the late 1980s by providing deficit targets, but its major failing involved its requirement of dramatic budget cutting on a regular basis. The Budget Enforcement Act of 1990, in contrast, keeps the deficit from getting worse than it otherwise would but requires not so much additional dramatic action, since controversial deficit reduction is in the law itself, along with extensive means of enforcement. To the extent that GRH paved the way for the 1990 law, it deserves credit. But the fiscal accomplishments of GRH itself in the late 1980s were meager.

It is hard to argue that GRH was essential for deficit reduction after 1985, because more substantial deficit cutting occurred earlier in the decade without the "spur" of GRH. Further, the $60 billion difference between the FY 1986 deficit of $221 billion and the $155 billion of FY 1989 resulted largely from economic expansion and the growth of Social Security reserves.[68] Nor had conservative economic ideology triumphed in fiscal policy practice by late

1990. Phil Gramm admitted in 1989 that "we haven't had the fundamental reordering of priorities that I had hoped for."[69] His original cosponsor, Ernest Hollings, was harsher in judgement: "It's a sham. This thing that was intended as a sword and it's being used as a shield."[70] Once the targets were met on paper for the fiscal year, additional spending could proceed.

The failure of GRH from 1985 to 1989 was of two sorts. It first failed to provide adequate sanctions to curb the political routines of budgeting. Once the courts struck down the GAO role, the OMB as a direct agent of the president could figure the numbers as expediency required. The deeper problem was that both the president and Congress preferred expedience, for their fiscal priorities had not changed. Deficit reduction was not highest on either list of values until George Bush demonstrated a newfound resolve in 1990.

The second failure was its assumption that a specific economic ideology would be self-imposed by the legislature and produce new forms of behavior. One could not expect a conservative economic ideology to bind a Democratic Congress. Though many in the party had repudiated Keynes in practice, they had not changed their views on the size of government or on the need for redistribution (just review the questionnaire results from 1986 in chapter 2). The "party of government" would find ways to protect its programs. Many Republicans had their own tax expenditures and spending programs (defense, farm price supports) to defend.[71] Widespread support for Phil Gramm's economic ideology would never appear in practice.

One might view this as a simple triumph of interests over broader fiscal theories. Interest dominance of Congress is a recurrent theme among political scientists. Theodore J. Lowi argues that "congressmen are guided in their votes . . . by whatever organized interests they have taken as most legitimate and that is . . . the only necessary guideline for the framing of laws."[72] But the situation is a bit more complicated than this stark characterization suggests. Program defense by Democrats and Republicans resulted from their personal allocative and distributive convictions as well as their need to service interests back home for electoral gain. Lawmakers had beliefs congruent with local interests due to recruitment processes; representation worked. So pure interest did not simply overrun all ideological conviction to produce deficits, but rather constituency interests in tandem with lawmakers' closely-held beliefs in parts of the budget prevailed over concern about the whole. Legislators' policy goals were primary, and they were representative. "Responsible opinion" of the political stratum often mistook this for a triumph of pure interest over the common good, particularly because the stratum's stabilization prescriptions were ignored.

Congress did demonstrate indifference in practice, if not in word, to stabilization strategy until 1990. Only White House persistence kept them on track toward a multiyear deficit reduction plan in that year. Though lawmakers from 1985 to 1989 gave lip service to worries from the political stratum about the deficit, agreement on the smaller measures necessary to reduce it substantially seldom happened. Despite growing trade and currency problems, the economy chugged along at a moderate growth rate, permitting fiscal politics in Washington to focus on battles over tax increases (macroallocation) and program spending (microallocation and distribution). The clear exception to this pattern was the October 19, 1987 crash, but the financial shakeup had no marked effect upon the macroeconomic course of succeeding months. Thus budgeting returned to its traditional "micro" focus; compromises varied incrementally from previous budgets in aggregate, leaving deficits hovering around $150 billion. In the absence of a clear constituency-based demand for fiscal change a la 1981, only economic urgency or presidential insistence could restore the "big picture" to budget debates.[73]

Is a long-term solution at hand? The prospect remains unclear. Congress may find ways to evade the discipline of 1990, and the White House may yet abet their efforts. Deficit reduction is agreeable to all in the abstract. But lawmakers' convictions and constituents tend to converge on the currency of the institution—particular spending and tax programs. This puts the onus of flexibility on the president, who likewise may prefer emphasizing budget parts over a solution for the whole. All could fall back on rationalizations of culpability that remained eminently defensible, logically and empirically. The sky had not fallen and others could be blamed.

A breakthrough in the impasse could occur in one of four

ways. First, elections could restock the legislature with enough lawmakers having ideology and supporting constituencies compatible with the president's views to produce consensus. Second, a president could be elected whose economic ideology comported with the political economy of a majority in Congress. Third, immediate economic peril threatening to sink the president and Congress could force a grand compromise. Finally, the president could change his convictions about the means of deficit reduction. In mid-1990, George Bush pursued this final option. It was the only realistic way out at the time.

CHAPTER 6

Conclusion

Lawmakers value their convictions. Some convictions are immutable, some are vaguely held, some change from month to month. In this web of positions one can find a definable pattern of thought with direct consequences for actions. Allocation, distribution, and stabilization attitudes define for legislators the "fiscal good," the desirable direction of national policy in the budget process. Budget politics in the 1980s was a major battle over the public interest, conducted in public debate.[1] That is to the good. But most have found the results wanting; budget policy from 1979 to 1989 is widely regarded as a failure. Open debate about closely held convictions does not necessarily produce good policy, in this instance because the reasons for budget frustrations have to do with how the context of debate shaped its substance. Members' collective norms and the electoral process that placed them in Washington in the first place tilted discussion in the direction of unsuccessful outcomes.

These attributes of institutional structure in effect tolerated and encouraged deficits by inhibiting initiatives of a scale necessary to solve the problem. Only in 1990 did presidential resolve overcome such constraints, but by only a narrow margin, at substantial political cost to the chief executive, and with uncertain ultimate results.

THE FISCAL GOOD

Every lawmaker's definition of the fiscal good arises not from disembodied cerebration but in reference to concrete political and institutional circumstances. Specifically, recruitment processes and reelection worries constitute primary influences upon budget thinking and voting. Patterns of recruitment create lasting policy boundaries for legislators, a restriction they accept willingly, for their convictions usually fit easily within the limits of acceptability for their supporting electoral coalitions. Lawmakers think over whether or not a vote has appreciable electoral impact; if not, constraints upon their choice are eased. The currency of electoral success is denominated in programs, so members quickly learn to "think small" in budgeting and focus more energy on specific aspects of authorizations, appropriations, and reconciliation than on budget resolutions.

Important congressional norms, including specialization, reciprocity, and accommodation, are also grounded in incentives produced by electoral arrangements.[2] One specializes in programs dear to one's beliefs and one's district. Even the question of the fiscal "big picture" is delegated to a few specialists—the Budget committees and Joint Economic committee—whose efforts are noted by their peers primarily when they threaten the "small picture" of committee specializations and district concerns. Most legislators are inevitably "detail people" whose careers can be measured in individual policy victories and defeats of modest scale. Political trading over bits can get each bargainer a satisfactory part of a larger bill. Chamber rules are tools of combat over such matters; the legislative schedule discourages serious reflection on issues other than those of the moment. And the issues of the moment usually concern programs.

Defining the fiscal "good" in this environment requires clear program convictions, flexible stabilization principles, and some knowledge of what has happened in the economy lately. The good is comprised mainly of opinions about programs—both allocative ("Should the federal government do this?") and distributive ("Does it promote equity?")—and stabilization tactics of the short-run. It also includes views about the overall size of government, totems to which legislators have long publicly subscribed. Immediate economic events occupy and motivate the lawmakers. Broader theories of how to stabilize the economy in the long-term receive little attention or articulation in Congress.

Though this style of fiscal thinking seems set by stable environmental characteristics, fiscal convictions in Congress do vary over time. Legislators, however fuzzily and tentatively, often rethink their views on budget policy in response to external conditions, usually by revising their definition of the correct immediate tactics. Three forces tend to stimulate the rethinking that goes on: economic events, agenda setting by the political stratum, and election results. The first two encourage individual members to ruminate on their substantive commitments, while the latter changes collective deliberations by altering who occupies Capitol Hill and the White House.

AGENTS OF CHANGE

The major forces of change in the 1980s were electoral: the Republican victory of 1980, the 1982 Democratic comeback in the House, and the election of George Bush in 1988. One result was the dominance in 1981 of new fiscal ideas of uncertain merit that ended up contributing to the deficit. Another was the onset of a period of "divided government" after 1982, producing problems of governance well described by James Sundquist: "If the president sends a proposal to Capitol Hill . . . the opposition-controlled House or houses of Congress—unless they are overwhelmed by the president's popularity and standing in the country—simply must reject it. Otherwise they are saying the president is a wise and prudent leader."[3]

White House budgets received routine rejection after 1982. Reagan and his antitax pledge, however, remained popular enough to raise the political costs of aggressive pursuit of deficit reduction for Democrats or "responsible" Senate Republicans. The legislature's posture toward the executive grew defensive since Reagan was far more inclined to cut domestic programs than was the vast majority of Congress. All this made persistent, huge deficits more likely. George Bush provided a stark contrast to his predecessor in 1990. He pursued long-term deficit reduction as a top priority and proved flexible on its specifics.

But Congress did make some progress in deficit reduction before 1990, albeit with much wailing and gnashing of teeth. They managed to do so without hitting domestic spending programs hard again after 1981, and despite a reluctant White House. One reason for the progress was the insistent pressure from the political stratum—national media, economic and Washington "expert" opinion—claiming the onset of economic perdition if deficit-cutting did not commence immediately. The legislature skirted further cuts in domestic programs in the early 1980s and found savings through a myriad of small tax increases and very selective shaving of entitlements. But room for this maneuver began to run out by 1985 when the political stratum's demands for cuts butted against the domestic program commitments of lawmakers. The result was the gimmickry of Gramm-Rudman-Hollings.

The political stratum can act as an agent of change, but its effectiveness is far more circumscribed than is that of elections or economic events. It has clout in that politicians, particularly budget captains, "pay close attention to their peer groups of Washington influentials, the media and policy experts."[4] So practical theories and the latest stabilization ideas gained the attention of lawmakers through the intermediaries of the political stratum, making these elites the prime conveyors of gloom and doom scenarios as deficits persisted. But the link of the political stratum with local electorates is nil. As one senator said to me: "Responsible opinion in Washington is not at all the same as the concerns of my constituents. And I am paid to represent the latter, not the former." When the sky did not fall, the urgency of appeals for action became less arresting. But the stratum could always press for basic fiscal responsibility, and on this score, legislators were understandably defensive and unwilling to ignore the pleas.

The limited effect of the political stratum is bad in that it contributed to the persistence of large deficits that may impede the long-term performance of our economy and make fiscal discipline even harder to muster in the future. The limited effect of the political stratum is good in that lawmakers represented their constituents, who were less convinced of the end of the world and more concerned with their programs, in refusing to follow the political stratum's call to action. And in the short term, it was the public that was right and the political stratum that was wrong. No one said that representation would be pretty; the structure of our electoral system provides for this fragmented kind of responsiveness on major issues that national elites seldom can disrupt.

The political stratum may plead for movement, but nothing concentrates a lawmaker's mind on the future more than serious economic problems in the present. Events had their sharpest immediate impact in 1981 and 1987. Without high inflation and unemployment engendering a sense of crisis, the new president's program would not have rushed through Congress as it did. The stock market crash of 1987 roused Congress and the president from entrenched and hostile positions by raising the specter of a major economic downturn unless deficit reduction occurred soon. These situations revised practical theories, reshaped stabilization tactics, and temporarily restored focus upon the bigger problem of stabilization strategy.

What did not happen in the economy also explains much of the policy course of the decade. Moderate economic growth accompanied by trade and budget deficits produced macroeconomic worries but little sense of immediate calamity. Economic recovery buoyed Reagan's popularity, making his veto threats and no-new-taxes pledge an insuperable obstacle for any deficit solution acceptable to Congress, which in turn deferred the broader problem in the interest of programmatic compromise. The cushion of favorable economic performance, however, did permit a gradual and piecemeal reduction of the deficit in 1982 and 1984. When out-year deficits no longer seemed likely to balloon, in large part because of frozen defense spending, the legislature and president after 1985 tolerated deficits of about $150 billion annually. Gramm-Rudman-Hollings became a means for postponing hard choices.

The limited progress points up the shortcomings of elections and economic events as agents of change in congressional budgeting. Elections can bring in enough new legislators to shift the balance of fiscal opinion, as did the Republican gains in 1980 and the Democratic gains in the House in 1982 and Senate in 1986. But new legislators quickly manifest the style of fiscal thought found among their older colleagues. Changing congressional membership mainly alters the programmatic mix of preferences in the institution, but offers little likelihood of a legislative initiative in the direction of overall fiscal policy. The only policies providing actual long-term fiscal change in recent years came from the White House in 1981 and 1990. Elections are most consequential to fiscal policy in determining the resident of the White House.

Economic problems can cause a temporary loosening of program commitments for the "greater good," permitting responsiveness to a strategic approach from the president should he be fortified by public popularity. The economic calamities of 1980–81 hardly reconstituted the framework of congressional fiscal thinking, but did make members receptive to new fiscal approaches from a White House with political momentum. The year 1987 likewise witnessed no such transformation in legislative thought, but its crisis atmosphere produced a greater degree of reciprocal "give" on specific taxes and spending than had been usual between president and Congress earlier in the decade.

Gramm-Rudman-Hollings did promise a congressional stabilization strategy and straightforward annual tactics in the form of deficit targets. But its consideration and implementation were showcases of political maneuvers aimed at undercutting the law. The 1987 amendments postponed serious deficit reduction for several years and left a huge amount of "wiggle room" when defining whether a target was in fact achieved. Ultimately, neither elections, economic reversals, the pleading of the political stratum, nor a fiscal process gimmick like GRH could transform the political economy of the legislature or the rigidity of the president. Unless the chief executive can lead Congress toward a more far-reaching deficit solution than it can construct through its own internal bargaining, only unforeseen acts of God or the economy can force substantial cuts in the deficit.

What makes the president the prime mover in deficit reduction? The chief executive is more able to follow long-term stabilization objectives than the fragmented Congress, and can resolve fiscal squabbles with remarkable speed—by changing his mind, as George Bush did in 1990. Presidents probably know less about programs than the average member of Congress, and it is easier to simplify your approach to deficit reduction if you are simpler in your understanding and allegiance to parts of the budget. This alone is no guarantee that a sound fiscal course will be trumpeted from the White House, as the decade of the 1980s vividly demonstrates. But the possibility of constructive action seems greater in an institution where one potentate focuses on the whole than in an institution comprised of 535 barons obsessed with parts.

THEORETICAL CONTEXT

It remains to place this case study into theoretical perspective and garner some lessons about the limits and possibilities of Congress. I have demonstrated that legislators have a serious interest in the public good, as defined by economic ideology and practical theories, that orients much of their behavior. This fact does not comport well with either of two major theories of political economy that base their explanations of fiscal events upon deductive postulates. One, the theory of public choice, introduced in chapter 5, holds that microeconomic motives explain the budget actions of Congress.[5] Another, academic Marxism, examines congressional actions from a class perspective.[6] Each follows a similar explanatory procedure: (1) salient concepts of human nature and behavior are asserted, (2) a particular situation is analyzed from the perspective of such concepts and (3) the concepts are found to explain the fundamental aspects of the behavior examined.

This type of explanation can illuminate aspects of congressional fiscal action, but it suffers from two defects that limit its utility. First, by attributing narrow motives to politicians, it shrinks the world of politics to an analytically manageable size and in so doing limits our understanding of political possibility. Second, it denies that we can understand what politicians are doing by reference to their own thoughts and explanations; rather, the noises of officeholders mask the grander reality. Legislatures are supposedly less about policy argument than they are about market-type transactions or class conflict.

Consider in this context public choice theory. Buchanan and Wagner describe their model as "not at all complex, and it offers satisfactory explanations" of the recent fiscal record.[7] Lawmakers are assumed to be vote-maximizers, voters benefit-maximizers, and bureaucrats power-maximizers, leading to deficit financing as an endemic feature of national fiscal policy. Legislators bear primary guilt for deficit spending, as they distribute benefits to garner votes. Unfortunately, acceptance of this model requires the dismissal of certain inconvenient facts. The argument "ignores both the fact that until 1980 the public debt as a percentage of GNP fell steadily throughout the postwar period and the fact that Congress seldom increases expenditures or cuts taxes much beyond what the president proposes."[8] Fiscal politics is simply more complex than the model asserts.

James Buchanan has admitted the limited explanatory utility of the model in a recent article.[9] The advent of deficits, he acknowledges, has not resulted from iron laws of self-seeking behavior, but rather due to a "breakdown in moral constraints."[10] These constraints are "the product of biological evolution, cultural evolution, and possibly, rationally calculated moral pre-commitment."[11] Here is an admission that thoughts other than those deductively asserted by public choice models direct legislative behavior. Buchanan is correct in averring that pleasing constituents through spending does not constitute the universe of legislative motivations. Moral reasoning is complex; legislators define the fiscal good and bad variously and act accordingly. The desire to distribute benefits is only one current in a broad and complex flow of thoughts. One cannot understand the course of a river's channel by reference only to one of many powerful currents.

Marxist analysis is much more empirically elusive than that of public choice; practically any behavior in a capitalist society can be related in some way to its deductive categories. Once the material basis of human life is assumed, classes are introduced and declared antagonistic, and the role of the state, whether "relatively autonomous" or not, examined, explanations of deficits can be composed. One scholar of this persuasion to address deficits with particular thoroughness is James O'Connor in his *Fiscal Crisis of the State.*[12]

For O'Connor, the state in capitalist society has two main and often mutually contradictory functions: "accumulation and legitimation. This means that the state must try to maintain or create the conditions in which profitable capital accumulation is possible. However, the state also must try to maintain and create the conditions for social harmony" by preserving its popular legitimacy.[13] Governmental spending is of two functional sorts: social capital ("spending required for capital accumulation") and social expenses ("projects and services required to maintain social harmony").[14] Beginning in the 1970s, the state entered a period of fiscal crisis, defined as a tendency for state spending to outstrip its revenues. The state could not effectively discharge its accumulation and legitimation functions simultaneously. This meant that economic performance might founder and governmental legitimacy decline, as it did in the late 1970s. In this way, O'Connor claimed that the "theory of economic growth depends on class and political analyses of the determinants of the budget."[15]

A more empirical examination of fiscal politics calls into question this broad formulation. It cannot be disputed that national budgets reflect the configuration of social and economic power and status found within nations, but this occurs regardless of whether their means of production is publicly or privately owned. Further, actual governmental behavior fits Marxist categories at best roughly. As White and Wildavsky note: "The more empirical Marxist scholars become, the more they investigate specific decisions, the harder it is to distinguish their evidence from that of ordinary social science."[16]

Fred Block, seeking to justify more precisely than does O'Connor the "relative autonomy" of the state, argues that "ruling class members who devote substantial energy to policy formation become atypical of their class, since they are forced to look at the world from the perspective of state managers. They are quite likely to diverge ideologically from politically unengaged ruling class opinion."[17] Why use class categories to explain their behavior, then? For Block, such autonomy can never be divorced from class analysis—ultimately any explanation, to be true, must be framed by the proper deductive categories.

Another problem lies in the very definition of the state itself. How can one begin to define the multitudinous actors located in disparate institutional locations in Washington as a unified state unless they are all charged with some broad authority of "system maintenance"? But this is a duty discharged by every government in the world, and usefully so. To use the term "state" in this sense may be accurate, but has little to do with class analysis. To view the state as acting primarily in response to established power structures does not require that we first understand all such structures in a class framework. Such a deduction assumes legislators operate in a context to which they are oblivious and requires that we discount their expressed motives and reasons as not grounded in the ultimate reality of class relations. The analyst can then reduce discussion about government to matters of functional impact upon the processes of accumulation and legitimation in a capitalist polity. As with public choice theory, what lawmakers say they are doing is not what they are doing; only the deductive analyst knows with confidence what they are doing.

Both public choice and Marxist analysis underplay the importance of intentionality in legislative action. By intentionality I mean the concept that politics is driven by the conscious intentions of actors as evident in their speech and action. Legislative behavior is not easily captured by deductive generalization; careful empirical analysis requires that such broad conclusions be heavily qualified. Yes, members do like to keep monies flowing back home and are concerned about the interests of finance capital when making budget decisions, and the two theoretical approaches discussed above assist us in understanding these phenomena. Neither of these tendencies alone, though, explains the twisting fiscal course of the 1980s in Congress. The roots of legislative thinking and behavior are various, encompassing practical theories, ideological beliefs, and political calculations.

Public choice and fiscal crisis theory, by understating intentionality, manage to overstate the import of recent fiscal problems. Both suggest that fiscal imbalance is deeply rooted in the structure of the political system and that only drastic measures can solve it. The actual explanation is not so grand. Deficits can be traced to the intentions of an institutional actor, the president, and to the perception of political costs in the minds of legislators. In the 1980s political risks increased primarily due to the stubbornness of a popular president. The higher political costs—to ideology (good programs might be cut; bad taxes might be raised) and reelection—created protective motivations and brought on chronic deficits.

There is nothing deductively automatic about this. A legislative-executive budget accord to reduce the deficits remained possible throughout the 1980s, one that could have satisfied legislators' fears about reelection, soothed nervous capital markets, and ameliorated the fiscal problem simultaneously. Such an accord arrived in 1990; others may be possible (and necessary) in the future. One need not look to Marx or microeconomics for an explanation, but rather to the thought and actions of Ronald Reagan, George Bush, and the Congress.

Neither deductive approach allows the possibility that politics centrally involves the intentional pursuit of the public good.[18] In doing so, they deform political understanding and make less possible the pursuit of the good in public life. This is not to say that legislators are morally exalted, or make fewer mistakes than their constituents when arriving at decisions, or that they think through fiscal problems with any distinguishing clarity. But members of

Congress do pursue the fiscal good as each defines it, and acknowledging that can enhance our understanding of political possibility.

INSTITUTIONAL POSSIBILITY

Much of the criticism of Congress during the 1980s in effect asked legislators to be who they are not—elite analysts responding to conventional policy wisdom—instead of elected representatives. An examination of the political economy of legislators shows their fiscal concerns flow naturally from the duties of their jobs. One duty of representatives is to reflect opinions back home, and this lawmakers did relatively well, particularly in defending "their programs." The public wanted balance, but not at any price, and so did their representatives. The Burkean plea to regard the common interest above that of one's constituents is compelling, when such an alternative can be carefully crafted. It could not be carefully crafted during much of the 1980s because of the impediments of program politics and the confusion (and frequent error) in elite circles over the proper stabilization course. Legislators did not follow elite policy advice very well, but that advice was often wrong about the immediate effects of deficits.

Deficits persisted because accurate representation can lead, on its merits, to dubious policy. Collectively, lawmakers' intentions produced a large problem of policy choice. Students of public decisions often laud "policy rationality" in which the most efficient means to clearly ordered goals is employed. But how to order goals when they diverge on both the spending parts and fiscal whole? The only way to proceed is via politics. All that ensures, though, is that the decision made will satisfy a majority of legislators, on representative grounds, in which budget parts figure most prominently. Political rationality requires calculating political costs, which throughout the 1980s proved so sizeable that no attempt to put the parts into a package to move decisively toward budget balance could succeed.[19] Reducing red ink meant one had to compromise ideological beliefs, place at risk programs important back home, and challenge a popular president on revenues and spending. No wonder lawmakers sought out convenient rationalizations. Presidents can alter the cost calculations in favor of deficit reduction by threatening costs of their own as George Bush did in 1990.

Such instances are likely to be infrequent, though, because the political costs to presidents of such action can be great.

When considering fiscal possibilities, we need to comprehend the legislature's limits as an institutional policy-maker. Congress does not create much original policy, but it does process fiscal ideas coming from elsewhere. For those ideas to become law, they must seem better than the likely alternatives in constituency and programmatic terms and as stabilization tactics. We are left with a legislature driven by the substantive political economy of its members in a representative fashion, meaning an institution with a persistent bias toward programs. External events—economic change and elections—alter the mix of program preferences in Congress and make possible departures from that institutional fixation on programs.

Legislators think for themselves, act on what they think, and their actions have consequences. The fiscal limits of Congress are set by the ideas of its members. Identify limits and you have identified institutional capacity. To attain the good in public life, we need to comprehend what those we sent to Congress to secure it for us are contemplating. In their routines of thought lie our possibilities.

APPENDIXES

APPENDIX I

Congressional Interviews 1985–1987

The following list includes all legislators questioned, except for a small number wishing to remain totally anonymous. In 1985, eight Senators (6 R, 2 D) and twelve Representatives (8 D, 4 R), all members of the Budget committees, were questioned, along with sixty staffers of the Budget committees or its members. All but two of the personal budget staffers of committee members were interviewed during this time. Seventy nonspecialist House members were interviewed about their decisions on the FY 1987 budget resolution after the vote occurred on May 15.

Also questioned in 1986 were ten members of the House Budget committee (5 D, 5 R), one Senate Budget committee member, and nine nonspecialist Senators. In 1987, two more Senators were interviewed. Nonspecialist legislators were questioned about their voting on budget matters generally and the FY 1987 budget resolution in particular (see Appendix III), and also about their political economy if time permitted. Interviews with Budget committee members ranged more widely, from economic ideology and fiscal policy to the budget process and its politics.

Representatives

Butler Derrick*	D-S.Carolina	22 January 1985
Martin Frost*	D-Texas	23 January 1985
Willis Gradison*	R-Ohio	29 January 1985
James Jones*	D-Oklahoma	15 February 1985
Lynn Martin*	R-Illinois	19 February 1985
Ralph Regula*	R-Ohio	19 February 1985

153

Thomas Downey*	D-New York	28 February 1985
Bill Frenzel*	R-Minnesota	17 June 1985
Leon Panetta*	D-California	18 June 1985
Howard Wolpe*	D-Michigan	19 June 1985
Norman Mineta*	D-California	27 June 1985
Vic Fazio*	D-California	28 June 1985
Denny Smith*	R-Oregon	7 May 1986
Marvin Leath*	D-Texas	12 May 1986
Marty Russo*	D-Illinois	14 May 1986
Marjorie Holt*	R-Maryland	14 May 1986
John Spratt	D-S.Carolina	15 May 1986
Judd Gregg	R-New Hampshire	15 May 1986
Mark Siljander	R-Michigan	15 May 1986
Charles Stenholm	D-Texas	15 May 1986
Buddy Roemer	D-Louisiana	16 May 1986
Mickey Edwards	R-Oklahoma	16 May 1986
Harold Volkmer	D-Missouri	16 May 1986
Tom Hartnett	R-S.Carolina	16 May 1986
G. William Whitehurst	R-Virginia	19 May 1986
Nancy Johnson*	R-Connecticut	19 May 1986
Wayne Dowdy	D-Mississippi	19 May 1986
Gene Chappie	R-California	19 May 1986
Ed Jenkins*	D-Georgia	20 May 1986
Charles Bennett	D-Florida	20 May 1986
Doug Barnard	D-Georgia	20 May 1986
J. Alex McMillan	R-N.Carolina	20 May 1986
Bob Wise	D-W.Virginia	21 May 1986
Jim Cooper	D-Tennessee	21 May 1986
William Goodling*	R-Pennsylvania	21 May 1986
Mike Synar	D-Oklahoma	21 May 1986
Doug Bereuter	R-Nebraska	22 May 1986
Stan Lundine	D-New York	22 May 1986
Bob Livingston	R-Louisiana	22 May 1986
Hal Daub	R-Nebraska	23 May 1986
George Brown	D-California	29 May 1986
Tommy Robinson	D-Arkansas	3 June 1986
Robert Matsui	D-California	3 June 1986
Don Pease	D-Ohio	3 June 1986

Duncan Hunter	R-California	4 June 1986
William Hughes	D-New Jersey	4 June 1986
George Crockett	D-Michigan	5 June 1986
Stephen Neal	D-N.Carolina	5 June 1986
William Dannemeyer	R-California	5 June 1986
Sander Levin	D-Michigan	6 June 1986
Peter Kostmayer	D-Pennsylvania	6 June 1986
Vin Weber*	R-Minnesota	6 June 1986
Jerry Lewis	R-California	9 June 1986
George Wortley	R-New York	9 June 1986
Howard Neilson	R-Utah	9 June 1986
Robert Walker	R-Pennsylvania	9 June 1986
Matt McHugh	D-New York	10 June 1986
Morris Udall	D-Arizona	10 June 1986
Tim Penney	D-Minnesota	10 June 1986
Hank Brown*	R-Colorado	11 June 1986
Cooper Evans	R-Iowa	12 June 1986
Ben Erdreich	D-Alabama	12 June 1986
John Hiler	R-Indiana	12 June 1986
Jim Slattery*	D-Kansas	15 June 1986
Phil Crane	R-Illinois	17 June 1986
Bill Richardson	D-New Mexico	17 June 1986
Bruce Morrison	D-Connecticut	17 June 1986
Lane Evans	D-Illinois	18 June 1986
James Olin	D-Virginia	18 June 1986
Dick Armey	R-Texas	19 June 1986
Esteban Torres	D-California	19 June 1986
Robert Dornan	R-California	19 June 1986
Anthony Beilenson	D-California	20 June 1986
Jim Moody	D-Wisconsin	23 June 1986
James Oberstar	D-Minnesota	24 June 1986
Frank Guarini	D-New Jersey	24 June 1986
Doug Bosco	D-California	24 June 1986
Joe Kolter	D-Pennsylvania	25 June 1986
Jim Bates	D-California	25 June 1986
Doug Walgren	D-Pennsylvania	25 June 1986
Chris Perkins	D-Kentucky	26 June 1986
Robert Lindsay Thomas	D-Georgia	26 June 1986

Claudine Schneider   R-Rhode Island   30 June 1986
Sherwood Boehlert   R-New York   15 July 1986
Steve Bartlett   R-Texas   15 July 1986
Major Owens   D-New York   16 July 1986
Harris Fawell   R-Illinois   16 July 1986
Richard Durbin   D-Illinois   17 July 1986
Richard Ray   D-Georgia   17 July 1986
John Kasich   R-Ohio   18 July 1986
John Porter   R-Illinois   30 July 1986

Senators
Mark Andrews*   R-N.Dakota   1 February 1985
Nancy Kassebaum*   R-Kansas   7 February 1985
Charles Grassley*   R-Iowa   28 February 1985
Robert Kasten*   R-Wisconsin   8 March 1985
Slade Gorton*   R-Washington   17 June 1985
James Sasser*   D-Tennessee   26 June 1985
J. Bennet Johnston*   D-Louisiana   26 June 1985
Carl Levin   D-Michigan   2 May 1986
Rudy Boschwitz*   R-Minnesota   8 May 1986
Max Baucus   D-Montana   3 June 1986
William Proxmire   D-Wisconsin   4 June 1986
Dennis DeConcini   D-Arizona   6 June 1986
Alan Cranston   D-California   19 June 1986
Thad Cochran   R-Mississippi   24 June 1986
John Melcher   D-Montana   27 June 1986
Dave Durenburger   R-Minnesota   15 July 1986
Alan Simpson   R-Wyoming   18 July 1986
Pete Domenici*   R-New Mexico   23 February 1987
William Roth   R-Delaware   27 February 1987

---

*Present or past Budget committee member.

APPENDIX II

Stratification Sample for 1986 House Nonspecialist Interviews[1]

	Democrats			
	Northeast	South	Middle West	West
Percentage of all				
House Democrats	22	40	21	17
Sample quota	9	16	9	7
Number interviewed	9	16	9	7
	Republicans			
	Northeast	South	Middle West	West
Percentage of all				
House Republicans	22	26	29	24
Sample quota	6	8	8	7
Number interviewed	6	8	8	7

[1]Democrats comprised 41 of the 70 sampled (59%); they totaled 253 of 435 in the House in 1986 (58%). Republicans totaled 29 in the sample (41%) and 182 in the 1986 House (42%).

APPENDIX III

Question Schedule for 1986 Nonspecialist Interviews

1. What considerations played a role in your vote on final passage of the FY 1987 budget resolution?
   Probe: policy—constituency—D.C. influence concerning resolution overall or its parts
2. Do you expect that similar or different considerations will play a role in your vote on the reconciliation bill this year?
   Probe: policy—constituency—D.C. influence concerning bill overall or its parts
3. How did Gramm-Rudman-Hollings affect the way you approached the vote on the FY 1987 resolution?
4. How is a resolution vote different from other sorts of roll calls? How is a reconciliation vote different? An approprations vote?
5. What are your views about the proper role of the national government in the economy?
   Probe: % GNP a concern?

Favor income maintenance/progressive taxation?
Annual balanced budget a necessity?
6. How did you develop these views?
7. How do you view the present state of the national economy?
   What are your short-term expectations for it? Long-term
   expectations?
8. How do you view the present state of your district's (state's)
   economy? What are your short-term expectations for it? Long-
   term expectations?

APPENDIX IV

1986 Questionnaire to House and Senate Offices[1]

1. How influential were each of the following upon *your member's* vote on final passage of
   the budget resolution on May 15, 1986? (Please circle the correct response.)

	Very influential		Somewhat influential		Not at all influential	
Constituents	5	4	3	2	1	0
House party leaders	5	4	3	2	1	0
Lobbyists	5	4	3	2	1	0
Staff	5	4	3	2	1	0
The president	5	4	3	2	1	0
Gramm-Rudman-Hollings act	5	4	3	2	1	0
Personal convictions	5	4	3	2	1	0
Budget committee chair or ranking member	5	4	3	2	1	0
Budget comm. members	5	4	3	2	1	0
Other representatives	5	4	3	2	1	0

2. Please circle the appropriate response for the following statements, indicating whether
   your member would

   Strongly Agree, Agree, Neither agree nor disagree,
   Disagree or Strongly Disagree with them.

A. Congressional party leaders should work more actively to build support for budget resolutions.	SA	A	N	D	SD
B. National government spending at present consumes too large a percentage of the GNP (currently 24%).	SA	A	N	D	SD
C. The national government should balance its budget every year.	SA	A	N	D	SD
D. The Gramm-Rudman-Hollings act promotes responsible deficit reduction.	SA	A	N	D	SD

E. The Gramm-Rudman-Hollings act should be
repealed.   SA   A   N   D   SD
F. The national government should reduce inequality
in private income through taxation and spending.   SA   A   N   D   SD
G. Defense spending in real terms should be frozen or
reduced in the FY 1987 budget resolution.   SA   A   N   D   SD
H. Revenue increases should be included in the FY
1987 budget resolution.   SA   A   N   D   SD

3. Which of the following does *your member* think are having the strongest influence on the course of the economy at present? (Circle one or more.)

a. interest rates   d. oil prices
b. budget deficits   e. balance of trade deficit
c. tax policy   f. stock and bond markets
                         g. other (specify) _____

4. Which of the following does *your member* think are the major problem areas of the economy at present? (Circle one or more.)

a. productivity growth   d. interest rates
b. inflation   e. balance of trade deficit
c. budget deficits   f. unemployment
                         g. other (specify) _____

5. What does *your member* think
economic conditions will be   Good   Uncertain   Bad
—nationally, over the next   Don't
12 months?   5   4   3   2   1   0   Know
—nationally, over the long
term (1 to 5 years from   Don't
now)   5   4   3   2   1   0   Know
—in the home district, over   Don't
the next 12 months?   5   4   3   2   1   0   Know
6. What is *your member's* view of
the current economic condi-   Don't
tions in the home district?   5   4   3   2   1   0   Know

[1]Budget assistants were identified in all House and Senate offices and received the questionnaire.

NOTES

CHAPTER 1

1. The classic study of this sort in John Kingdon's *Congressmen's Voting Decisions* (Ann Arbor: University of Michigan Press, 1989), now in its third edition, and based on interview data collected in 1970. Though numerous studies have relied upon elite interviews, the decreasing accessibility of legislators in recent years has prevented more systematic sampling of congressional opinion.

2. The concept of "political stratum" is nicely delineated in Joseph White and Aaron Wildavsky, *The Deficit and the Public Interest* (Berkeley: University of California Press, 1989), pp. 412–29.

3. Allen Schick, *Crisis in the Budget Process: Exercising Political Choice* (Washington: American Enterprise Institute, 1986), pp. 42–43.

4. This emphasis can be found in a number of works about budgeting in the 1980s: Allen Schick, *Congress and Money* (Washington: Urban Institute, 1980); idem, "The Evolution of Congressional Budgeting," in Alan Schick, ed., *Crisis in the Budget Process* (Washington: American Enterprise Institute, 1986); Lance LeLoup, *Budgetary Politics*, 3rd ed. (Columbus, Ohio: King's Court, 1986); Howard E. Shuman, *Politics and the Budget*, 2nd ed. (Englewood Cliffs, N.J.: Prentice-Hall, 1988); Aaron Wildavksy, *The New Politics of the Budgetary Process* (Glenview, Ill.: Scott Foresman, 1987); John P. Gilmour, *Reconcilable Differences* (Berkeley: University of California Press, 1990). Two more recent works— Joseph White and Aaron Wildavsky, *The Deficit and the Public Interest* (Berkeley: University of California Press, 1989) and Alan Schick, *The Capacity to Budget* (Washington: Urban Institute, 1990)—discuss legislative thinking and institutional consequences more thoroughly than the others.

5. There is also, of course, a distinctive product known as a continuing resolution. This is usually an omnibus appropriations bill passed as a stopgap measure when Congress has not been able to meet its budget obligations on time. The fact remains that major changes in program budgeting and fiscal policy of a lasting sort are first declared in resolutions and then enacted through enforcement of a reconciliation bill. See Stanley E. Collander, *Guide to the Federal Budget: Fiscal Year 1987 Edition* (Washington, D.C.: Urban Institute Press, 1985).

6. John B. Gilmour, *Reconcilable Differences* (Berkeley: University of California Press, 1990), p. 157.

7. White and Wildavsky (1989) and Schick (1990) analyze this occurrence in detail.

8. See M. Stephen Weatherford and Lorraine M. McDonnell, "The Role of Presidential Ideology in Economic Policymaking," *Policy Studies Journal*

12:691–702 for a discussion of the components of economic ideology. Richard A. and Peggy B. Musgrave, *Public Finance in Theory and Practice,* 2nd ed. (New York: McGraw-Hill, 1976) detail the components of fiscal policy.

9. The goal typology comes from Richard Fenno, *Congressmen in Committees* (Boston: Little, Brown, 1973). It was also employed by John Kingdon in his book *Congressmen's Voting Decisions,* 3rd ed. (Ann Arbor: University of Michigan Press, 1989).

10. See Kingdon (1989) for more elaboration on these goals.

11. The interviews were completed during two time periods. From January through March of 1985, I interviewed 8 members of the Senate Budget committee (6 R, 2 D) and 12 members of the House Budget committee (8 D, 4 R), along with staff of all committee members and 8 committee staffers. From March 1986 through February 1987, I interviewed 93 lawmakers. These included 70 non-specialist (nonBudget committee member) Representatives, organized into a sample stratified by party and region (41 D, 29 R), who were questioned shortly after their vote on the FY 1987 budget resolution. Though the sample could not be random, proportional representativeness concerning party and region was achieved. In addition, I interviewed 10 nonspecialist Senators and 2 Republican members of the Senate Budget committee during this time, as well as 11 additional members of the House Budget committee (5 D, 6 R). As this chapter makes clear, the large majority of members preferred to be interviewed on the record. The questionnaire was mailed to all House offices, and personally delivered to all Senate offices. A total of 253 House and 67 Senate responses resulted. Budget staffers of legislators received the questionnaire and completed them. More detail on the personal interviews and questionnaire is included in the appendixes, as is a copy of the questions asked in each. This chapter is a summary of the findings, presented thematically. More detailed empirical findings are included in the next chapter.

12. Jerrold Schneider, *Ideological Coalitions in Congress* (Greenwood, Conn.: Greenwood Press, 1978), pp. 11–12.

13. Musgrave and Musgrave (1976), chap. 1–2.

14. Ibid., p. 7. Stokey and Zeckhauser define six reasons for market failure. They are: imperfect flow of information, transaction costs, the nonexistence of markets for some goods, market power, externalities, and public goods. See Edith Stokey and Richard Zeckhauser, *A Primer for Policy Analysis* (New York: Norton, 1978), chap. 14.

15. Weatherford and McDonnell, "The Role of Presidential Ideology in Economic Policymaking," p. 83.

16. Quoted in David Stockman, *The Triumph of Politics* (New York: Harper and Row, 1986), p. 315.

17. Musgrave and Musgrave (1976), p. 6.

18. The major reversals suffered by Democratic party leaders in the early 1980s are discussed in chapters 2 and 3.

19. Musgrave and Musgrave (1976), p. 6.

20. See Kingdon (1989).

21. White and Wildavsky (1989), p. 352.

22. The term was first coined by Edward Tufte in his book *Political Control of the Economy* (Princeton: Princeton University Press, 1974).

23. See Allen Schick, *Congress and Money* (1980) and Steven E. Schier,

"Thinking about the Macroeconomy: The House and Senate Budget Committees in the 1980s" (Washington: American Academy of Higher Education, 1986).

24. This is discussed in greater detail in chapter 3.

25. See Robert D. Reischauer, "Getting, Using and Misusing Economic Information," in Allen Schick, ed., *Making Economic Policy in Congress* (Washington: American Enterprise Institute, 1983), pp. 214–46.

26. Further discussion of this can be found in chapter 4.

27. For example, see John Kingdon, *Congressmen's Voting Decisions,* 3rd ed. (Ann Arbor: University of Michigan Press, 1989); Aage Clausen, *How Congressmen Decide: A Policy Focus* (New York: St. Martin's, 1973); Donald Matthews and James Stimson, *Yeas and Nays* (New York: Wiley, 1975).

28. Arthur Maass, *Congress and the Common Good* (New York: Basic Books, 1982).

29. Ibid., p. 28.

30. Ibid., p. 5.

31. Darrell West, *Congress and Economic Policymaking* (Pittsburgh: University of Pittsburgh Press, 1987) demonstrates this point for the budget votes of 1981.

32. Kingdon (1989), chapter 1.

33. Ibid., chapter 10.

34. My interviews with 70 Representatives yielded only 4 who failed to state a personal policy conviction in response to my question: "What considerations were important for you in deciding how to vote on the FY 1987 budget resolution?" See note 31, chapter 2, for a more complete breakdown. Analysis of the questionnaires sent to legislative assistants in chapter 2 indicates that convictions were the most important influence upon the votes of Representatives and Senators on this resolution. The 70 are termed "nonspecialists" because none had served on the Budget committee, the formulator of the resolution.

35. This finding is also consistent with that of David Kozak in his analysis of budget voting around 1980. See his *Contexts of Congressional Decision Behavior* (Lanham, Md.: University Press of America, 1984).

36. Though members regularly referred to a budget resolution as a "big picture" or "philosophical" vote, their views of reconciliation bills were more variable. Some viewed it as a philosophical test similar to that of a resolution. Others saw it, in the words of Representative John Kasich (R-Ohio) as a very "complicated" vote that did not admit to a stable decision pattern because "you deal with programs in detail with that as well as with the budget overall." Most, however, mentioned it in the same breath with appropriations bills as a tool for helping out particular interests. A representative response came from House member John Spratt (D-S.Car.) who claimed that "you have to view reconciliation like an appropriations bill. It is a complex bill and programs affecting all sorts of interests are affected by it."

37. Theoretically, appropriations could be cut by a reconciliation bill, if the bill were passed near the beginning of the next fiscal year, October 1. The 1974 budget act provided for this possibility. In practice, appropriations have not been affected by reconciliation, in part because they have been late in passing Congress. See Allen Schick, *Reconciliation and the Congressional Budget Process* (Washington: American Enterprise Institute, 1981).

38. Allen Schick, *The Capacity to Budget* (Washington: Urban Institue, 1990), p. 179.

39. White and Wildavsky (1989) argue this convincingly.

40. Richard Fenno, *Congressmen in Committees* (Boston: Little, Brown, 1973).

41. See John Kingdon (1989), chap. 3.

42. Chapters 2 through 5 demonstrate this in detail.

43. Steven E. Schier, "The Political Economy of Congressional Budget Voting," paper presented at the annual meetings of the Northeastern Political Science Association, Boston, November 13–17, 1986.

44. On this point, see Allen Schick, *Congress and Money* and *The Capacity to Budget;* Aaron Wildavsky, *The New Politics of the Budgetary Process;* Joseph White and Aaron Wildavsky, *The Deficit and the Public Interest;* John Gilmour, *Reconcilable Differences.*

45. John Gilmour (1990) discusses this process further on pp. 134–38.

CHAPTER 2

1. For example, on political calculations re voting, see Kingdon (1989); on empirical policy assessments, see Reischauer, "Using and Misusing Economic Information"; on ideology, see Jerrold Schneider, *Ideological Coalitions in Congress* (Westport, Conn.: Greenwood Press, 1978).

2. Leon Festinger, *A Theory of Cognitive Dissonance* (Evanston: Row, Peterson, 1957), p. 13.

3. By this, I mean that they had never been members of the Budget committee, since my primary focus involved budget resolutions and reconciliation legislation.

4. James Thurber of American University and I jointly conducted the questionnaire research. Specifically, the questionnaire was delivered personally to the legislative assistants for budget issues of Senators and via mail to those of Representatives. Unlike West (1987), we decided not to assume that submitting a questionnaire to an office produced a valid and reliable measure of legislators' attitudes unless the appropriate staffer completed the questionnaire. Legislators are far too busy to bother with such matters. Our technique, while not perfect, gives a more systematic picture of the pattern of opinions than possible from elite interviews alone. The response rate is respectable for the House and quite high for the Senate.

Questionnaires were delivered in May and June of 1986, addressed the legislative assistants in charge of budget matters, whom in all instances we had previously identified by name. Usable responses came from 67 Senate offices and 253 House offices, for respective return rates of 67% and 58%. The results of the survey were representative by party in the Senate (54% Republican, 36 of 67) and roughly so in the House (54% Democratic, 136 of 253, compared to 58% of the actual House). Results of certain parts of the survey also are consistent with my findings from personal interviews with 70 House members during this time period, as is noted later in the text.

5. It is important to note that budget projections are extremely sensitive to assumptions about national economic conditions. If unemployment is 1% higher than estimated, for example, federal spending increases by some $30 billion.

Assumptions about interest rates also have very large effects on budget calculations; the lower the projected rate, the lower the deficit estimate. This is because
by 1990, 16% of annual spending involved interest payments on the national
debt. As interest rates rise, so do debt payments.

6. White and Wildavsky (1989) make this point on p. 509.

7. This generalization may seem sweeping, but it is thoroughly documented
in White and Wildavsky (1989).

8. Fiscal committees are defined as tax, Appropriations, or Budget committees. Significant patterns were absent concerning economic ideology, practical
theories, and political influences on the FY 1987 budget resolution vote. As will
be noted later, the overwhelming majority of legislators found personal convictions to be most important on the vote, perhaps explaining the lack of variation.
The absence of variation by fiscal committee status in practical theories and
economic ideology reflects the representativeness of those committees overall in
reference to the chamber membership, and the possibility that any attitudinal
effects of specialization appear primarily at the program level, rather than in
reference to broader economic concerns. Keep in mind also that analyzing seniority, region, and fiscal committee status while controlling for party does produce
small numbers of cases in some instances, thus reducing the probability of finding
significant relationships.

9. This series of events is chronicled fully in the next chapter. See also Darrell
West, *Economic Policymaking in Congress* (Pittsburgh: University of Pittsburgh
Press, 1986).

10. Though Table 2–1 deals only with regional and party groupings, a
similar pattern of opinions divided members ideologically, as measured by ADA
scores, annual scores of each member of Congress by the Americans for Democratic Action. A score of zero indicates total conservatism, 100 total liberalism.
Annual scores for each legislator since 1981 were summed and averaged to come
to this calculation.

11. *Congressional Record,* 7 November 1985, p. H9866.

12. Consider the following examples. Representative Connie Mack (R-Fla.)
to Dr. Albert Sommers, chief economist of the Conference Board: "I get the sense
of what you are saying is that the real question is what is going to happen to
interest rates. That this would be the most significant impact on the future of the
budget and the deficits. Is that true? . . . Would you be a little more specific for
me as to what you would do to keep interest rates at a low level?" (House Budget
Committee, *Hearings on the FY 1984 Budget,* 10 February 1983, p. 37). Representative Pat Williams (D-Mont.) to Richard Rahn, chief economist of the Chamber of Commerce of the United States: "Is the present deficit acting as a stimulant
or a depressant now in the short run, say twelve to fifteen months?" (House
Budget Committee, *Hearings on the FY 1984 Budget,* 23 February 1983, p. 78.)
Senator Slade Gorton (R-Wash.) to Alexander Trowbridge, National Association
of Manufacturers, Dr. Jack Carlson, National Association of Home Builders, and
Peter Herder, National Association of Home Builders: "I would like each of you
to comment on would you favor an attack on budget deficits, yes or no. . . . If you
do favor it, in theory, at what level do you favor it, the President's $100 billion
over three years, Senator Dole's $150 billion over three years, or some larger
figure than that?" (Senate Budget Committee, *Hearings on the FY 1985 Budget,* 7
February 1984, p. 383). Senator Lawton Chiles (D-Fla.) to Stanley Fischer, professor of economics at MIT: "How in the hell do you get those interest rates

down?" (Senate Budget Committee, *Hearings on the FY 1984 Budget,* 16 February 1983, p. 489.)

13. *Congressional Record,* 4 October 1985, S12629.

14. Ibid., 11 December 1985, H11880.

15. House Budget Committee, *Hearings on the FY 1984 Budget,* 3 February 1983, p. 211.

16. Democratic and Republican views on welfare are discussed in the context of budget debates in the ensuing chapters.

17. See "After Long, Bruising Battle, House Approves Welfare Bill," *Congressional Quarterly,* 19 December 1987, pp. 3157–58.

18. Ibid., 1 May 1981, H8152.

19. Ibid., 4 May 1983, S5912.

20. Ibid., 10 October 1985, S13073.

21. This is only one of several indicators conservatives referred to in order to illustrate the size of government, but it was the indicator brought up most frequently. The percentage of GNP taken in taxes and the spending trend since 1981 also occupied their attention. The common theme, regardless of the indicator chosen, was that government at present is too large.

22. Ensuing chapters demonstrate the differing views of allocation in the budget debates of the 1980s.

23. The following articulate but inaccurate prediction by Ways and Means member Robert Matsui (D-Calif.) in mid-1986 is illustrative: "At present, crude oil prices are down, interest rates have stabilized, and frankly I can't understand why auto sales are so strong. The economy will hold up pretty well, but we will have a recession within twenty-four months because our expansion has lasted over two years. A natural cyclical contraction is bound to occur. We will blame the recession on the deficit, which we blame for all our ills. Germany and Japan may help to minimize the recession by helping to minimize the trade problem so that we can export more. The deficit won't get us into the recession, but it will impede our way out, and the recession could kill Gramm-Rudman-Hollings as a practical piece of legislation."

24. Robert D. Reischauer, "Getting, Using and Misusing Economic Information," in Allen Schick, ed., *Making Economic Policy in Congress* (Washington: American Enterprise Institute, 1983), pp. 214–46.

25. *Congressional Record,* 4 May 1981, H8356.

26. Ibid., 4 May 1983, S5969.

27. White and Wildavsky (1989) make this point on p. 548.

28. Roger H. Davidson, *The Role of the Congressman* (New York: Pegasus, 1969), p. 121.

29. Of the 70 Representatives in my interview sample, only some 17% (12) were uniformly locally-oriented on budget issues. The remainder either possessed mixed local-national or national orientations. This may understate the number of locally-oriented legislators in the House as a whole, since these members probably would be less likely to grant me an interview.

30. See Kingdon (1989), chapters 9–12.

31. The findings of the questionnaire research corroborate the following tabulation of personal interview findings. The following table presents the responses of 70 Representatives in May, June, and July 1986 to the question: What considerations were most important to you in deciding how to vote on the budget resolution for FY 1987?

	Northern Democrats (N = 25) %	Southern Democrats (N = 16) %	Republicans (N = 29) %	Overall (N = 70) %
Personal convictions	100	100	87	95
Constituents	59	53	26	45
Other legislators	41	53	26	45
Party leaders	26	27	13	21
Staff	11	20	10	12
Administration	—	—	6	3

32. Kingdon (1989), chap. 10.

33. Richard Fenno, *Home Style* (Boston: Little, Brown, 1978) and Kingdon (1989), chap. 2.

34. Kingdon (1989), chap. 2.

35. See note 31.

36. Kingdon (1989), p. 45.

37. Robert A. Bernstein, *Elections, Representation, and Congressional Voting Behavior* (Englewood Cliffs, N.J.: Prentice-Hall, 1989), p. 102.

38. Ibid., pp. 44–45.

39. It is important to note that lawmakers have a finely developed set of perceptions about their constituency. They know best and are most concerned about the views of their supporting electoral coalition. For members of Congress, "constituencies are complex bundles of attentive and active elites. Constituents' intensities count for as much as their numbers, and members have rather good ways to gauge intensities and reflect them in decisions" (Kingdon, 1989, xii).

40. Fenno (1978).

41. Gary Jacobson, *The Politics of Congressional Elections* (Boston: Little, Brown, 1987).

42. Kingdon (1989), chap. 5.

43. As they did in the personal interviews, not meriting enough mentions to be included in the tabulation listed in note 31.

44. West (1987).

45. Schick (1990), p. 173.

46. George Bush in 1990 reversed himself and pushed for higher taxes as part of a 5-year, $500 billion, bipartisan deficit reduction package. Bush exercised influence in a negative fashion throughout the turbulent negotiations over a deficit-reduction package by allowing a government shutdown through his veto of a continuing resolution and by threatening to veto a package with elements not to his liking. Bush got his compromise but lost public popularity in the process. Democrats roasted him for refusing higher taxes for the rich, and his prolongation of the crisis seemed to suggest executive weakness. Real deficit reduction had big political costs. George Bush was willing to pay them; Ronald Reagan was not.

47. Though a few Republicans mentioned that they liked to support the White House "when they could," no legislator of either party in my 70 interviews mentioned the president or his staff as major influences on their FY 1987 resolution votes. This probably reflects the plan of the White House to avoid lobbying on budget issues until the autumn appropriations round, but the absence of administration stature is striking. See the tabulation in note 31.

48. See corroborating evidence in the tabulation of personal interview responses in note 31.

49. Chapters 3 through 5 explain this in detail.

50. Aaron Wildavsky, *The New Politics of the Budgetary Process* (Glenview, Ill.: Scott, Foresman, 1987), p. 200.

51. On the new oligarchy, see Lawrence C. Dodd and Bruce I. Oppenheimer, "Consolidating Power in the House: The Rise of a New Oligarchy," in Dodd and Oppenheimer, eds., *Congress Reconsidered* (Washington: Congressional Quarterly, 1989), pp. 39–64. White and Wildavsky (1989) also make this general point throughout their book.

52. See the tabulation of personal interview responses in note 31.

53. See the tabulation of personal interview responses in note 31.

54. Kingdon (1989), chap. 7.

55. None of the Budget committee members of either party I interviewed in 1985 and 1986 expressed confidence in the budget analysis performed by OMB. The only variance was in the vehemence of the criticism, which usually differed along partisan lines. With the passage of Gramm-Rudman-Hollings I and II, however, the OMB role in estimating deficit targets grew and became tightly delimited by law. This no doubt reduced legislative skepticism about the OMB discharge of that particular duty. For additional analysis of the role of CBO, OMB, and staff on a resolution vote, see chapter 5.

56. Peter Goldman, "The Reagan Steamroller," *Newsweek*, May 11, 1981, p. 39.

57. Festinger (1957), p. 3.

58. Ibid., p. 13.

59. Ibid., p. 7.

60. Ibid., p. 16.

61. Ibid., p. 21.

62. Ibid., p. 25.

63. Recorded in M. Spiro, "Ghosts: An Anthropological Inquiry into Learning and Perception," *Abnormal and Social Psychology* 48: 376–82.

64. Of course, some legislators may have thought they were voting for large deficit reduction each year, given the substantial numbers bandied about by those negotiating annual deals, but even the most simple-minded learning process by the middle of the decade would produce the conclusion that such efforts were not enough, and lead to skepticism about any deficit reduction numbers appended to current legislation.

65. White and Wildavsky (1989), p. 426.

66. For empirical data on this, see White and Wildavsky (1989), pages 232 and 424–25.

67. For a probing analysis of the tensions over economic policy encountered by state legislators and how they seek to resolve them, see William K. Muir, *Legislature: California's School for Politics* (Chicago: University of Chicago Press, 1982), pp. 48–55.

CHAPTER 3

1. As one Democratic senator related to me: "In 1981 around here everyone was worried about economic chaos—we were in a rough economic period. Sure

each person had programs to protect, but the pressure was on to do something dramatic about the economy."

2. Jonathan Rauch, "The Fiscal Ice Age," *National Journal,* 10 January 1987, pp. 58–64.

3. White and Wildavsky (1989), p. 35. See their book, pages 333–43, for an excellent analysis of the origins of the deficit problem. A similar analysis can be found in Schick (1990), p. 198.

4. On this, see Allen Schick (1980), and Lance T. LeLoup, *The Fiscal Congress* (Greenwood, Conn.: Greenwood Press, 1980).

5. See Schick (1980), LeLoup (1980), and John W. Ellwood and James A. Thurber, "The New Congressional Budget Process: The Hows and Whys of House-Senate Differences," in Lawrence C. Dodd and Bruce I. Oppenheimer, eds., *Congress Reconsidered* (New York: Praeger, 1977), pp. 188–215.

6. *Congressional Record,* 30 April 1979, H9041.

7. Ibid., 12 May 1980, S10866.

8. These included a minority substitute by Delbert Latta, ranking Budget committee member, providing more for defense, an $8.4 billion cut in outlays, and a $6.5 billion revenue reduction (*Congressional Record,* 3 May 1979, H9032), an amendment by Ralph Regula (R-Ohio) and Marjorie Holt (R-Md.) to cut spending (9 May 1979, H10484), a proposal by John Rousselot (R-Calif.) to balance the budget while providing $16 billion in tax cuts, and one by Jack Kemp (R-N.Y.), requiring $6 billion in domestic cuts and a 10% tax cut to offset bracket creep (10 May 1979, H10655).

9. One came from Senator Orrin Hatch (R-Utah), and the other from Senator William Armstrong (R-Colo.). See the *Congressional Record,* 5 and 6 May, 1980.

10. Ibid., 5 May 1980, S9804.

11. See Allen Schick, *Reconciliation and the Congressional Budget Process* (Washington: American Enterprise Institute, 1981).

12. A study that demonstrates public opinion leaned in this direction in 1980 is W. E. Miller and J. M. Shanks, "Policy Directions and Presidential Leadership: Alternative Interpretations of the 1980 Presidential Election," *British Journal of Political Science* 12:299–356.

13. For example, see Allen Schick, "In Congress Reassembled: Reconciliation and the Legislative Process," *PS* 14:748–51; William Greider, *The Education of David Stockman and Other Americans* (New York: Dutton, 1982); David Stockman, *The Triumph of Politics* (New York: Harper and Row, 1986); Howard Shuman, *Politics and the Budget,* chap. 9; Lance T. LeLoup, "After the Blitz: Reagan and the U.S. Congressional Budget Process," *Legislative Studies Quarterly* 7:321–39; Paul Craig Roberts, *The Supply-Side Revolution* (Cambridge: Harvard University Press, 1984); James D. Savage, *Balanced Budgets and American Politics* (Ithaca: Cornell University Press, 1988), chap. 7.

14. This is a central finding of Darrell West's book, *Congress and Economic Policymaking.*

15. Stockman (1986), pp. 90–130.

16. Kingdon in *Congressmen's Voting Decisions* demonstrates how both can occur simultaneously. See his chapters on the consensus mode of decision.

17. Arthur Laffer in "Analyzing Supply-Side Economics: A Symposium," in Thomas J. Hailstones, ed., *Viewpoints on Supply-Side Economics* (Reston, Va.: Reston Publishing, 1982), p. 70.

18. David Raboy, "Norman B. Ture on Supply-Side Economics," in Thomas J. Hailstones, ed., *Viewpoints on Supply-Side Economics,* p. 67.

19. For a good summary of these tenets, see Ronald A. Krieger, "Supply-Side Economics: An Introduction," in Thomas J. Hailstones, ed., *Viewpoints on Supply-Side Economics,* pp. 49–61.

20. Paul Craig Roberts in "Analyzing Supply-Side Economics: A Symposium," in Thomas J. Hailstones, ed., *Viewpoints on Supply- Side Economics,* pp. 77–78.

21. The Carter administration's endorsement of this approach is evident in the *Economic Report of the President 1981* (Washington: Government Printing Office, 1981).

22. Jude Wanniski, "An Authentic Guide to Supply-Side Economics" (Memorandum, A. B. Laffer and Associates, Rolling Hills Estates, Calif., 1980), p. 2.

23. Stockman (1986), p. 237.

24. Ibid.

25. Ibid., pp. 59–60.

26. Ibid., p. 50. The political cachet of these tactics was inescapable to a candidate in search of popular support and convinced of the need for smaller government.

27. This is all well described in White and Wildavsky (1989), p. 170.

28. Leonard Silk, "On the Supply-Side," in *Reagan the Man, the President* by Hedrick Smith et al. (New York: Macmillan), pp. 57–62.

29. Greider (1982), p. 140.

30. Ibid., p. 152.

31. Ibid., p. 151.

32. Ibid.

33. The administration eventually settled for a diluted form of Kemp-Roth. The actual tax cut passed into law in 1981 provided for a 23% across-the-board reduction in personal marginal income tax rates over 3 years. Cutting differing tax brackets by equal percentages produced a much larger dollar benefit for high income taxpayers, as Democrats pointed out in the 1981 congressional debates. This, along with the domestic program cuts proposed by the administration, became a central distributive issue of 1981. See Shuman, *Politics and the Budget,* pp. 262–67.

34. "Current services" is a budgeting term for the amount of spending necessary to keep programs operating at levels identical to that of the previous fiscal year. See Stanley Collender, *The Guide to the Federal Budget Fiscal 1987* (Washington: Urban Institute, 1986).

35. Appropriations are annual and multiyear allocations of funds for programs; authorizations set legal maximums for program spending in any given fiscal year. See Collender (1986).

36. Both Stockman (1986) and Roberts (1984) describe this process, and place blame squarely on each other for what went wrong.

37. Stockman (1986), p. 97.

38. Consider the following statement by Treasury Secretary Donald Regan before the Senate Budget committee in 1981 concerning the economic model employed for their forecasting: "The model we are using is a rational expectations model and a monetary model; it is not Keynesian." Keynesian economics assume that expectations change adaptively—that is, slowly over time—in response to actual changes in economic policy as opposed to rapidly in response to statements

of governments (Senate Budget Committee *Hearings*, 1 April 1981, p. 49).

39. White and Wildavsky (1989) make this point on p. 209.

40. A budget resolution is divided into 21 functional categories, 18 of which involve specific policy areas. Examples are function 050, defense; 350, agriculture; 570, medicare, and so forth. See Collender (1986).

41. Gilmour (1990), p. 14.

42. Stockman (1986), p. 176.

43. White and Wildavsky (1989), p. 117.

44. Stockman (1986), pp. 230–55.

45. Ibid., pp. 202–27.

46. White and Wildavsky (1989), p. 155.

47. David Mayhew (1974) terms this time-honored practice "credit claiming."

48. Fiorina (1977) claims pork barreling consumes an increasing amount of congressional time and energy.

49. See Kingdon (1989), chap. 2.

50. A sampling of the deals made can be found in Stockman's *Triumph of Politics* (1986), pp. 179–268, and in "White House's Lobbying Apparatus Produces Impressive Tax Vote Victory," *Congressional Quarterly*, 1 August 1981, 1372–73.

51. Dale Tate, "Reconciliation Conferees Face Slim Choices," *Congressional Quarterly*, 4 July 1981, p. 1169.

52. Stockman (1986), p. 228.

53. Shuman (1987), p. 268.

54. I am indebted to Joe White for providing evidence and analysis on this point. See the *CQ Almanac 1981* (Washington: Congressional Quarterly, 1982), pp. 98 and 100–101 for more details about how indexing was added.

55. Stockman (1986), pp. 266–76.

56. Ibid., p. 266.

57. House Budget Committee, *Hearings on the FY 1982 Budget*, 26 March 1981, p. 195.

58. *Congressional Record*, 12 May 1981, S9443.

59. Ibid., 7 May 1981, S8806.

60. A number of unsuccessful Senate amendments sought to reduce the rate of defense growth or protect spending for domestic programs. The Congressional Black Caucus sponsored an alternative budget resolution on the House floor, which cut defense by $2 billion but provided for a $56 billion tax cut and a balanced budget in FY 1982. David Obey (D-Wis.) proposed a liberal alternative budget allowing for an increase in defense spending and domestic spending, and a tax cut delayed until 1983. Both plans lost overwhelmingly.

61. *Congressional Record*, 7 May 1981, H8928.

62. For a description of the safety net, see Stockman, (1986), p. 130. For a Republican defense of the safety net on the House floor, see Eldon Rudd (R-Ariz.) in the *Congressional Record*, 30 April 1981, H8020.

63. *Congressional Record*, 4 May 1981, H8378.

64. Ibid., 7 May 1981, S8804.

65. Ibid., 11 May 1981, S9189.

66. House Budget Committee, *Hearings on the FY 1982 Budget*, 3 March 1981, p. 365.

67. *Congressional Record*, 30 April 1981, H8006.

68. House Budget Committee, *Hearings on the FY 1982 Budget,* 3 March 1981, p. 370.

69. *Congressional Record,* 12 May 1981, S9412.

70. Ibid., 1 May 1981, H8175.

71. For example, see the lengthy statement by Augustus Hawkins (D-Calif.) in the *Congressional Record* of 30 April 1981, H8160.

72. Ibid., 1 May 1981, H8154.

73. Ibid., 7 May 1981, H8918.

74. Ibid., 7 May 1981, H8989.

75. Ibid., 7 May 1981, H8903.

76. Ibid., 7 May 1981, H8930.

77. See Paul Courant and Edward Gramlich, *Federal Budget Deficits: America's Great Consumption Binge* (Englewood Cliffs, N.J.: Prentice-Hall, 1985), chap. 3–6.

78. See the statement by Ted Weiss (D-N.Y.) in the *Congressional Record,* 1 May 1981, H8148, for an example.

79. Darrell West (1987), p. 75.

80. Ibid., p. 43.

81. Ibid., p. 78.

82. Ibid., p. 80.

83. Ibid., p. 82.

CHAPTER 4

1. This analysis derives from an excellent treatment of the subject by White and Wildavsky (1989) on pp. 332–45.

2. John L. Palmer, "The Hidden Story of the Deficit," typescript, reveals how Congress took some steps to tame the deficit during this time.

3. Mark Kamlet, David C. Mowery, and Tsai Tsu Zu, "Whom Do You Trust: An Examination of Congressional and Executive Economic Forecasts," *Journal of Management and Policy Analysis* 6:365–84.

4. For further information on the inaccuracy of assumptions employed by CBO, OMB, and Congress in its budget resolutions, see the text of the Grassley speech (2 May 1984, S5177–79); Jonathan Rauch, "CBO's Wishful Thinking," *National Journal,* 7 March 1987, 550–54; Mark Kamlet, David C. Mowery, and Tsai Tsu Zu, "Whom Do You Trust: An Examination of Congressional and Executive Economic Forecasts," *Journal of Management and Policy Analysis* 6:365–84. See also the CBO *Economic Outlook 1986–90,* Appendix H, in which CBO admits that its forecasting errors are "quite large, a reflection of the limitations of economic forecasting generally."

5. The notable exception to the trend found in Table 3–1 is the administration forecast for 1984, created under the guidance of Martin Feldstein, Murray Weidenbaum's successor as head of the Council of Economic Advisors. Feldstein (with Stockman's support) sought to create assumptions more "realistic" than those promulgated during the first 2 years of the Reagan presidency. In doing so, he produced a rarity—a forecast more pessimistic than subsequent events.

6. Schick (1990), p. 138.

7. White and Wildavsky (1990), p. 353.

8. Senate Budget Committee, *Hearings,* 27 July 1982, pp. 21–22.

9. Senate Budget Committee, *Hearings on the FY 1984 Budget,* 3 February 1983, p. 177.

10. *Congressional Record,* 4 May 1983, S5950.

11. Ibid., 3 May 1983, S5863.

12. See Palmer, "The Hidden Story of the Deficit," typescript.

13. White and Wildavsky (1989) outline the various congressional factions on pp. 209–11.

14. White and Wildavsky (1989), p. 527.

15. Ibid.

16. Stockman (1986), p. 310.

17. *CQ Almanac 1982* (Washington: Congressional Quarterly, 1983), p. 187.

18. The reform was the result of the successful deliberations of a bipartisan presidential commission; substantial reductions in current benefit levels were not recommended by the commission. This explains the bipartisan support for the reform. See Paul C. Light, *Artful Work: The Politics of Social Security Reform* (New York: Random House, 1985).

19. John Palmer, "The Hidden Story of the Deficit," typescript.

20. Joseph White, "What Budgeting Cannot Do: Lessons of Reagan's and Other Years," 1987, typescript, p. 5.

21. See Joseph White, "What Budgeting Cannot Do," p. 6, for more detail on this point.

22. I interviewed 11 legislators with membership on both the Budget and a taxation or spending committee, and found no exceptions to this generalization.

23. Stanley E. Collender, *The Guide to the Federal Budget Fiscal 1986* (Washington: Urban Institute, 1985), p. 44.

24. Office of Management and Budget, *Budget Fiscal Year 1983* (Washington: Government Printing Office, 1982), pp. 3 and 22–23.

25. Administration resistance to tax increases derived from a belief that Congress had failed to cut spending as promised in reciprocity for the 1982 tax increase. Tables produced by the Senate Budget committee documenting the 1982 agreement indicated that approximately $3 in spending would be cut in 1982–84 for every $1 in revenue raised. This "three for one" swap was soon to find a prominent place in the budget lore of the White House. As Joseph White points out, however, most of the savings were to come from interest payment assumptions and management efficiencies over which Congress did not have direct jurisdiction. Reagan stuck to this proportion, however, in subsequent years to blame Congress for reneging on spending restraint. It served to increase White House intransigence in budget negotiations after 1982. See Joseph White, "What Budgeting Cannot Do: Lessons of Reagan's and Other Years," 1986, typescript, p. 5.

26. David Stockman, *The Triumph of Politics* (New York: Bantam Books, 1987), postscript, as reprinted in the *Congressional Record,* 7 January 1987, E87.

27. *Congressional Record,* 4 April 1984, H2304.

28. Ibid., 18 August 1982, S10765.

29. For examples of redistribution arguments, see Pat Williams (D-Mont.) of the House (4 April 1984, H2319) and Orrin Hatch (R-Utah) of the Senate (17 May, 1984, S5970).

30. House Budget Committee, *Hearings on the FY 1984 Budget,* 2 February 1983, p. 44.

31. For example, see his speech in the *Congressional Record*, 11 May 1983, S6509.

32. See Senator John Tower's comments at a Senate Budget committee hearing on March 3, 1982, for example. Senate Budget Committee, *Hearings on the FY 1983 Budget*, 3 March 1982, p. 52.

33. *Congressional Record*, 4 May 1983, S5928.

34. Ibid., 25 May 1982, H2745.

35. Ibid., 2 May 1983, S5767.

36. For example, see in the House debates, Wright, 24 May 1982, H2752; Lowry, 23 March 1983, H1592; Weber, 5 April 1984, H2382; in Senate debates, Gorton, 2 May 1984, S5397; Exon, 1 May 1984, S5108.

37. White and Wildavsky (1989), p. 387.

38. Congressional Budget Office, *An Analysis of the President's Budgetary Proposals for Fiscal Year 1984* (Washington: Government Printing Office, 1983), p. 17.

39. For example, see statements by Senator Bill Bradley (D-N.J.) (21 May 1982, S5875–76) and Representative James Martin (R-N.C.) (24 May 1982, H2674–75).

40. House Budget Committee, *Hearings on the FY 1983 Budget*, 17 February 1982, p. 111.

41. *Congressional Record*, 2 May 1983, S5760.

42. For explanations of these events, see Paul Courant and Edward Gramlich, *Federal Budget Deficits: America's Great Consumption Binge* (Englewood Cliffs, N.J.: Prentice-Hall, 1985), chapters 2, 3, and 4, and Alan Blinder, *Hard Heads Soft Hearts* (Reading, Mass.: Addison-Wesley, 1987), chapters 2 and 3.

43. *Congressional Record*, 16 May 1984, S5808.

44. For example, see Kassebaum, 2 May 1984, S5180, and Melcher, 11 May 1983, S6492, in the Senate; Daschle, 23 March 1983, H1613, in the House. See also Schier (1986) for a discussion of these concerns among members of the Budget committees.

45. House Budget Committee, *Hearings on the FY 1983 Budget*, 9 March 1982, p. 1.

46. *Congressional Record*, 26 April 1984, S5111.

47. Ibid., 5 April 1984, H2436.

48. See Jones, 4 April 1984, H2274, in the House; Evans, S5181, and Baucus, S5186, 2 May 1984, in the Senate.

49. See White and Wildavsky (1989), p. 353, on this problem.

50. Kemp in 1982 proclaimed: "I am against raising any taxes. There is no economic theory of any sort that advocates raising taxes in a recession" (25 May 1982, H2799). Senator Mattingly in 1983 argued: "Raising taxes at the beginning of an economic recovery is counterproductive, senseless and irresponsible" (23 June 1984, S8974). Cyclical argument was clearly the hard-liners forte.

51. Wright's comments occurred at a 17 February 1982 hearing of the House Budget committee. See House Budget Committee, *Hearings on the FY 1983 Budget*, 17 February 1982, p. 17.

52. For a discussion of why Democrats thought a tax increase would be necessary, see James D. Savage, *Balanced Budgets and American Politics* (Ithaca: Cornell University Press, 1988), pp. 225–30.

53. Quoted in Savage (1988), pp. 224–25.

CHAPTER 5

1. For details on the 1985 budget process, see White and Wildavsky (1989), chapters 16–18.

2. *Congressional Record*, 1 August 1985, S10375–77.

3. Ibid., 23 May 1985, H3647.

4. White and Wildavsky (1989) elaborate on this concept on p. 427. Recall also the questionnaire results in chapter 1 indicating the economic importance lawmakers attached to deficits.

5. *National Journal*, 16 November 1985, p. 2575.

6. Jonathan Fuerbringer, "Plan to Balance U.S. Budget by '91 Delayed in Senate," *New York Times*, 5 October 1985, pp. 1, 3.

7. Representative Sam Gibbons (D.-Fla.), chair of the Trade subcommittee of Ways and Means, on the floor in 1985 summarized the practical theory in current fashion among the political stratum: "As we borrow far too much money, we vastly distort the value of our dollar as it relates to trade overseas, and we vastly underprice imports to America. There is no way, no way I say to my colleagues, that we can cure this until we first cure ourselves, and that is to cure our deficits. . . . It is that process of borrowing on American savings and then from foreigners that keeps driving up the value of the dollar, keeps driving down the cost of goods coming into our country and keeps driving up the cost of goods exported from our country" (*Congressional Record*, 23 May 1985, H643).

8. On the paradoxes of public opinion on fiscal policy during this period, see White and Wildavsky (1989), chapters 18 and 19.

9. Large deficits made necessary frequent revisions in the debt limit in the 1980s, as the national debt more than doubled from 1981 to 1987. This became an embarrassing episode for Republican Senate leaders, who had to convince their "hard core" conservatives to swallow hard and support the increases. The failure of the budget process in 1985 brought resistance to a head, as Rudman's speech indicates. If the debt ceiling was not raised, the government would effectively run out of money due to insufficient borrowing. Increases in the debt ceiling had to pass for government to function.

10. See "Balanced Budget Backers Lose on 201–199 House Vote," *Congressional Quarterly*, 17 March 1979, p. 440.

11. James Buchanan and Richard Wagner, *Democracy in Deficit: The Political Legacy of Lord Keynes* (New York: Academic Press, 1977), pp. 139–40.

12. Ibid., p. 175.

13. *Congressional Record*, 3 October 1985, S12568.

14. Hobart Rowen, "The Get Rid of Government Act," *Washington Post National Weekly Edition*, 18 May 1985, p. 6.

15. Divisions over economic ideology lay at the center of controversy over the balanced budget amendment in 1982. Proponents, including most Republicans and many moderate and conservative Democrats, wanted reduced overall allocation by the government and a balanced budget at all stages of the business cycle. Opponents were more skeptical of the imperative of less allocation and believed that discretionary deficits could be economically beneficial. The debate also hinged on the feasibility of the reform. Supporters of the amendment believed that the budget process had failed because it had yielded unacceptable policies. Nothing short of a constitutional rule could curb the spending appetite of elected politicians. Opponents saw means for mischief in the amendment, through in-

creased off-budget expenditures and incentives for new forms of government inter-vention not denominated in expenditures. The Senate passed an amendment by a 69–31 margin, two votes more than the necessary two-thirds, on August 4, 1982, after eleven days of debate. Then-Democratic Representative Phil Gramm led a movement to get 218 signatures on a "discharge petition" to force the House Judiciary committee to either act on the bill or report it to the floor. The House Democratic leadership expedited consideration of the amendment in order to deprive its supporters of time to coalesce. The amendment received 236 affirma-tive votes, 187 negative; 46 short of the necessary two-thirds. The amendment sought to reduce the allocation and stabilization duties of the national govern-ment. It contained five sections: (1) annual budgets must be balanced unless three-fifths of both chambers agreed to void this section for a given year; (2) the rate of increase in federal spending was tied to increases in GNP; (3) the amend-ment was waived while war was declared; (4) the public debt limit was fixed unless altered by three-fifths of both chambers; (5) it would take effect in the second fiscal year after ratification. See the *Congressional Record*, July 20–29, August 2–4, 1982, for the Senate debate; October 1, 1982, for the House debate.

16. The president was to be given authority to rescind spending unless Con-gress disapproved of the rescission within 45 days. This reversed the rescission provisions of the 1974 Budget act, which required congressional approval of any rescission proposal. The power would be used when quarterly estimates showed federal expenditures proceeding at a rate in excess of the totals in the budget resolution. The president could not, however, cut any program more than 20% or reduce the levels of entitlement spending. Budget chair Pete Domenici opposed the initiative on the grounds that it would produce procyclical results and that the estimates could never be reliably enough calculated (see *Congressional Record*, 16 November, S16331). The amendment was tabled, 46–43, the large number of votes on its behalf indicated rising congressional frustration over deficits and a willingness to consider process reforms as a way out of the problem.

17. The original bill was brief (less than 4 pages long) but breathtakingly sweeping in its prescription for fiscal policy and overhaul of the budget process. It established maximum deficit goals of $180 billion in FY 1986, declining $36 billion per year over 6 years to zero by FY 1991. At the time, CBO estimated the FY 1986 deficit at $175 billion, necessitating no immediate cuts. But the FY 1990 budget was forecast at $120 billion. To meet the challenge, the budget process would be speeded up. The president had to submit a budget achieving the deficit target within 15 days of the convening of Congress. Budget committees were to report resolutions within the target by April 15 (formerly the "deadline," fre-quently violated, had been May 15). Second resolutions would no longer be required, and no amendments increasing spending without providing offsetting reductions would be allowed. All committees then would be required to allocate budget authority and outlay maximums among their subcommittees congruent with the resolution totals; no new entitlement legislation was allowable unless it could be certified not to add to the deficit. Reconciliation legislation was to pass Congress by June 15. Alongside this process lay an elaborate scorekeeping and enforcement mechanism. OMB and CBO were to report estimates of real GNP growth and the coming year's deficit jointly by the beginning of each fiscal year. If they could not agree, a midpoint between their forecasts would be used. The president would receive this report and be responsible for issuing an "emergency order" detailing across-the-board cuts in all programs except Social Security

(which was exempted) if the deficit, according to the estimates, exceeded the target. This "sequestering" of funds would then cause the deficit to hit the mandated target. Up to half of the cut was to come from non-Social Security entitlements, but only to the point where COLAs were eliminated. The remainder would come from all other programs. Interest payments on the national debt would not be affected. The cuts would be calculated jointly by OMB and CBO. If the nation suffered from a recession, the president could delay implementation of the order for 30 days after the CBO-OMB deficit report. He could also suspend all or parts of the bill during a recession.

18. An additional discussion of this point is found in White and Wildavsky (1989), p. 456.

19. The caucus is ably described in Richard E. Cohen, "Balanced Budget Plan Forces House Democrats to Get Their Act Together," *National Journal*, 16 November 1985, p. 2588.

20. The two versions differed in most major respects. The House provided for lower deficit targets and a balanced budget by 1990, accepting the numbers proposed by Obey during the first conference. It also included a different "escape mechanism" during economic downturns. Deficit targets would increase if annual economic growth exceeded 3%, and decrease if it fell below 3%. In this way, the economic effects of the plan would not be "procyclical." The revised Senate plan of November 6, however, kept the targets fixed at $36 billion in reductions for each year until balance was achieved in 1991. It did, however, reduce the "allowable error" for FY 1986 from 7% of the target amount to 5%. The Senate allowed that if a recession was predicted or actually occurred, Congress by joint resolution could suspend all or part of the target provisions, but the targets in the Senate version could only be permanently altered by an amendment to the law. The weightiest political difference between the House and Senate involved the programs to be exempted from sequestration. The House removed 8 domestic welfare programs from the chopping block (AFDC, Supplemental Security Income, child nutrition, veterans' pensions and compensation, community and migrant health care centers, WIC, and commodity supplemental food programs) and placed Medicare and Medicaid in the category of indexed programs that would only lose their COLA increases in the event of a sequester, protecting them from large cuts. The House exemptions dictated that a larger share of any sequestration would come from defense than would be the case under the Senate version, which had exempted only Social Security and veterans' benefits. A number of institutional differences also distinguished the two plans. The House allowed CBO to calculate the exact cuts to be included in a sequester order, though "consultation" with OMB was required. House negotiators were leery of allowing OMB, "the president's children" (in the words of a Budget committee member), to have any authority over sequestration. The November 6 Senate plan sought to counter objections to OMB by providing that the CBO and OMB would both calculate sequester orders, and then submit them to the General Accounting Office (an agency of Congress), where they would be examined, revised, and a final "certified" version would be produced. Both of these formats brought charges of unconstitutionality. House members argued that the OMB as an executive agency could not make spending decisions; Senators argued that CBO alone could not enforce spending decisions upon the president. The federal courts would have to resolve that issue, and the chambers differed in how they wanted the courts to approach the law. The House authorized suits by members of Congress or other

affected parties, and defined sections of the law as "nonseverable"; if one provision were found unconstitutional, the entire law was void. The Senate version stated explicitly that provisions of the law were severable by the courts, and provided a "fallback procedure" should the sequestration process be found unconstitutional. In that event, CBO and OMB were to calculate a sequester order, and a special joint committee of Congress, made up of the two Budget committees, was to act on the order, submitting it for floor approval in each chamber. It then would be presented to the president for his signature.

21. By the time of final passage, the Balanced Budget and Emergency Deficit Control Act of 1985 was a measure of baroque complexity. It included the deficit targets of the original Senate bill: $171.9 billion for FY 1986, then $144 billion, $108 billion, $72 billion, $36 billion, and zero by FY 1991, set with a $10 billion overage allowable each year. CBO and OMB were to estimate the deficit for each coming fiscal year as well as quarterly economic growth rates. Whether or not a sequester was necessary and in what amount would depend upon their calculations. The agencies would also estimate the "current law" baseline to be used in figuring the cuts. If they differed on any of the above numbers, the estimates would be averaged. The actual automatic cuts would first be calculated by CBO and OMB separately, then reviewed by the Comptroller General, who would average any differences between them and certify a final plan. A fallback procedure provided that a special joint Budget committee meeting formulate, Congress approve, and the president sign a sequester order should the courts rule the original sequestration process unconstitutional. As the Senate had preferred, the recession escape hatch could not be opened easily. Sequestration could be suspended by a joint resolution only if CBO or OMB predicted two consecutive quarters of negative economic growth or the Commerce department reported actual growth of less than 1% for 2 consecutive quarters.

The House claimed victory on its major agenda item. Eight programs were exempted from automatic cuts: Medicaid, AFDC, WIC (a food program for women and children), Supplemental Security Income, food stamps, veteran's pensions and compensation, and child nutrition. In addition, 5 health programs (Medicare, veterans' health, Indian health, community health, and migrant health) could only be subject to a sequestration cut of 1% in FY 1986 and 2% in FY 1987 and thereafter. Reductions in the remainder of nondefense programs had to make up the remaining half of a sequester order; this portended huge cuts in the FBI, airport safety, and numerous other programs should a sequester ever occur. Special rules were put in place to allow a sequester for FY 1986 totaling a maximum of $11.7 billion to go into effect on March 1, a victory for the Senate. Expedited budget process rules also became law. Two were of particular significance. First, the timetable of the budget process was compressed, requiring the president to begin the process with a budget proposal by January 3, rather than the end of the month. Congress was to complete work on a budget resolution by April 15 (formerly May 15 for the first nonbinding resolution and September 15 for the second resolution); the House would complete work on all appropriations bills by June 30. The second resolution was finally abolished in law, long after it had expired in fact. The new calendar supposedly would place pressure on Congress to act with rare zeal in order to avoid a sequester. A special FY 1986 sequester timetable also provided for automatic cuts by March 1 if the legislature found itself overshooting the $171.9 billion target. A second major alteration gave the Senate Budget committee authority to reign in wayward appropriations. Section 302 of the 1974 Budget act allowed points of order against appropriations bills exceeding the budget resolution's limits. Section 310(d) of GRH stated that in the Senate, any measure (floor amendment) that increased spending above a subcommittee's 302 allocation was out of order, and that only 40 votes were necessary to sustain the point of order. This meant that any amendment to an appropriations bill that would push spending beyond the GRH limit would have to include offsetting reductions in other programs to prevent breaching the target, unless a full 60 votes could be mustered against a point of order. Life for spending claimants in the Senate appropriations process would be more vexing as a result. In the House, GRH made mandatory the heretofore advisory discretionary outlay targets under Section 302, making the Appropriations committee the locus of bargaining over how programs would be funded within the discretionary limits. See Aaron Wildavksy, *The New Politics of the Budgetary Process* (Boston: Little, Brown, 1988), pp. 253–58, for a discussion of what happened in the appropriations process as a result of this provision.

22. *Congressional Record,* 11 December 1985, S17383.

23. On collegial decision-making, see Steven S. Smith, "New Patterns of Decisionmaking in Congress," in *The New Direction in American Politics,* pp. 203–34, edited by John E. Chubb and Paul E. Peterson (Washington: Brookings, 1985).

24. *Congressional Record,* 9 October 1985, S12966.

25. Schick (1990), p. 205.

26. Ibid., p. 79.

27. White and Wildavsky (1989), p. 516.

28. In 1986 the joint committee did meet and report out a sequester plan. The report made no further progress in Congress once the Budget committees began assembling the reconciliation bill. See Helen Dewar, "Domenici Fears Collapse of Deficit Control Effort," *Washington Post,* 12 September 1986, p. 8.

29. Leon Panetta, Dear Colleague letter, 17 June 1986, "Gramm-Rudman: Where We Stand," photocopy.

30. A good summary of the budget gimmicks of this era can be found in Schick (1990), p. 205.

31. Stephen Gettinger, "Negotiators Adopt $12 Billion Deficit Reduction Measure," *Congressional Quarterly,* 18 October 1986, p. 2588.

32. Stephen Gettinger, "Deficit-Cutting Proposals Seek to Avoid Cuts," *Congressional Quarterly,* 20 September 1986, p. 2179.

33. For further information of the methodology employed, see chapter 2 and the Appendixes.

34. Supporters numbered 116 of 253 House respondents (who overall were a bit disproportionately Republican) and 39 of 67 Senate respondents.

35. Based on tabulation of ADA scores, annual scores of each member of Congress by the Americans for Democratic Action. A score of zero indicates total conservatism, 100 total liberalism. Annual scores for each legislator since 1981 were summed and averaged to arrive at this calculation. Presidential support was calculated by summing annual,*Congressional Quarterly* presidential voting support scores for each member since 1981 and averaging them. A t test is a significance test for the likelihood that chance error produced the difference between

two means. A probability of less than .05 means that there are fewer than 5 chances in 100 that such a difference in means could occur by chance.

36. Jonathan Fuerbringer, "Deficit Cuts: Less of a Bite," *New York Times,* 25 September 1987, p. 9.

37. See White and Wildavsky (1989), pp. 518–20.

38. David Phelps, "Packwood Says Chance to Improve Deficit Missed," *Minneapolis Star Tribune,* 7 December 1988, p. 7M.

39. The 1987 poll is disclosed in E. J. Dionne, Jr., "Poll Finds Reagan Support Down But Democrats Still Lacking Fire," *New York Times,* 1 December 1987, p. 1. For information on the muddled public opinion about deficits, see the annual volumes of *The Gallup Poll* by George Gallup (Wilmington, Del.: Scholarly Resources, 1982–86).

40. Important issues of the year found their way into the breach. Congressional attempts in the continuing resolution to reinstate the "fairness doctrine," abolished by the Federal Communications Commission, met with stout presidential resistance. A compromise on aid to the Nicaraguan Contras permitted the administration to spend $14 billion in aid in return for a guaranteed congressional vote in February 1988 on continuing that aid. See *Congressional Quarterly,* 26 December 1987, for more details.

41. See *Congressional Quarterly Almanac 1988* (Washington: Congressional Quarterly, 1989), pp. 193–99, for a summary of the events of 1988.

42. Jackie Calmes and John R. Cranford, "Bush, Democrats Face Off on Bill to Cut Deficit," *Congressional Quarterly,* October 7, 1989, p. 2613.

43. Ibid.

44. Ibid., p. 3221. Allen Schick (1990) nicely summarizes the program games played with reconciliation throughout the decade on p. 179—further evidence of the dominance of program orientation in budgeting despite deficits.

45. Though the amount of the deficit reduction of the package was estimated at $492 billion at the time of its passage, a later CBO estimate raised the total savings to $496 billion. See Robert Pear, "'91 Budget Deficit Will Set a Record, Congress is Told," *New York Times,* 7 December 1990, p. A1.

46. The Senate on June 14 passed a "policy neutral" budget setting last year's totals for spending, in order to allow the appropriations process to get underway, as it had in the House. By this time, a budget summit between the White House and congressional leaders was well underway. See Pamela Fessler, "Budget Negotiators Expected to Get Down to Cases," *Congressional Quarterly,* 16 June 1990, p. 1863.

47. Pamela Fessler, "Bush's Sudden Shift on Taxes Gets Budget Talks Moving," *Congressional Quarterly,* 30 June 1990, p. 2029. Related facts from my narrative come from 1990 issues of *Congressional Quarterly.*

48. Legislators who had never supported amendments of this sort in the past voted for this one out of growing frustration with persistent deficits. For more on this, see the *Congressional Record* for the House for 17 July 1990, and George Hager, "Balanced Budget Amendment Fails in House; Act OK'd," *Congressional Quarterly,* 21 July 1990, p. 2284.

49. A capital gains tax cut seeks to reduce the special tax paid by investors upon the sale of stock. Proponents of the reduction argue it will stimulate more investment and thus economic growth; opponents argue it is a tax break for those of high income, and therefore unfair.

50. Pamela Fessler, "Capital Gains Tax Cut Is Once Again Pivotal Issue in Deficit Bargaining," *Congressional Quarterly*, 22 September 1990, p. 2996.

51. For more details on this, see *Congressional Quarterly*, 3 November 1990, p. 3715.

52. Relatively noncontroversial were the $182 billion in defense cuts over five years. A whole host of specifics in the plan produced much wrangling; for details, see *Congressional Quarterly*, 6 October 1990.

53. George Hager, "Defiant House Rebukes Leaders; New Round of Fights Begins," *Congressional Quarterly*, p. 3187. For further illustrations, see the *Congressional Record* of 4 October 1990.

54. The Democratic plan would have imposed a 10% surtax on millionaires and raise the top annual rate to 33%, increased the alternative minimum tax rate to 25% and raised the wage cap for Medicare payroll taxes to $100,000. In addition, it junked the gas tax increase and greatly scaled back increased Medicare payments, as well as including a capital gains cut aimed specifically at middle-income taxpayers. See George Hager and Pamela Fessler, "Negotiators Walk Fine Line to Satisfy Both Chambers," *Congressional Quarterly*, 20 October 1990, p. 3484.

55. Ibid., p. 3483. For further illustrations, see the 16 October 1990 *Congressional Record*.

56. A few legislators did argue the various plans would amount to stabilization failure because they did not cut the deficit enough. An example is Ernest Hollings's speech on the Senate floor on October 8. See the *Congressional Record*, 8 October 1990, pp. S14730–31.

57. In contrast to the House plan, the Senate bill did not alter personal marginal income tax rates, but did reduce personal deductions for high income taxpayers. It included a 10 cent a gallon gas tax while the House had none, while, unlike the House, avoiding a capital gains cut. Overall, the House plan increased taxes on those making over $200,000 annually by 7.4%; the Senate plan upped them 3.7%. Both reduced taxes for those making under $20,000 annually. For an examination of differences, see *Congressional Quarterly*, 20 October 1990, pp. 3480 and 3481.

58. His rating fell from the mid-70s to the 50s probably because the chaos of October reflected badly on his leadership and because Democrats had tarred him as a "protector of the rich." See Richard Morin, "It Isn't That We Have to Pay; It's Just How Unfair It All Is," *Washington Post National Weekly Edition*, 15–21 October, 1990, p. 37.

59. George Hager, "Parties Angle for Advantage As White House Falters," *Congressional Quarterly*, 13 October 1990, p. 3391.

60. Actually, the previous tax system contained a "bubble" of a higher tax rate of 33% for moderately high incomes that phased back to 28% for the highest income taxpayers (those making approximately over $150,000 annually). The "bubble" was burst by placing a flat 31% rate on all single incomes over $49,200 and married incomes over $82,050. See Pamela Fessler, "This Year's Battle May Be Over, But the War Has Just Begun," *Congressional Quarterly*, 3 November 1990, p. 3715.

61. Ibid.

62. George Hager, "One Outcome of Budget Package: Higher Deficits on the Way," *Congressional Quarterly*, 3 November 1990, p. 3711.

63. A cap also existed for 1994–95, but this was an aggregate cap for all

three areas, allowing Congress to shift spending priorities among them.

64. The enforcement mechanism also includes a "look back" procedure for violations of either pay-as-you-go or the spending caps. If either limit is exceeded after the sequester date for a fiscal year, the required offsetting savings are achieved by lowering the next year's cap or pay-as-you-go limit by the amount of the breach. An excellent explanation of all this can be found in Richard Kogan, "The Budget Enforcement Act of 1990: A Technical Explanation," typescript, Washington, D.C., 1990.

65. For more on this, see Lawrence J. Haas, "New Rules of the Game," *National Journal*, 17 November 1990, p. 2793.

66. Congressional Budget Office, *The Economic and Budget Outlook: Fiscal Years 1992–1996* (Washington: Government Printing Office, 1991), p. xiv.

67. On this, see Louis Uchetelle, "Experts Expect Stimulus to Economic Morale but Little Else," *New York Times*, 26 October 1990, p. All, and Lawrence J. Haas, "Beyond the Deficit," *National Journal*, 1 December 1990, p. 2940, and Robert Pear, "'91 Budget Deficit Will Set a Record, Congress is Told," *New York Times*, 7 December 1990, p. A1.

68. Jackie Calmes, "Gramm-Rudman-Hollings: Has Its Time Passed? *Congressional Quarterly*, October 14, 1989, p. 2684.

69. Ibid.

70. Ibid.

71. Theodore J. Lowi, *The End of Liberalism* (New York: Norton, 1980), chapter 3.

72. Ibid., p. 51.

73. GRH did produce some smaller effects worth noting, however. Budget "scorekeeping" by OMB and CBO probably did produce greater deficit reductions than might otherwise have been the case—reconciliation in 1986 and 1987 was reworked in order to hit the target as defined by the "green eyeshade" agencies. Other provisions that altered Senate rules gave new "bite" to budget procedures. For example, the Senate was not able to consider appropriations bills until after final passage of the budget resolution. Nongermane amendments to reconciliation legislation were prohibited. Limits fixed by the budget resolution upon subcommittee appropriations totals meant that no amendment to an appropriations bill could raise spending unless it specifically cut spending elsewhere or raised revenues. Overriding this rule required 60 votes; it did not happen in 1986 or 1987. See Aaron Wildavsky, *The New Politics of the Budgetary Process* (Boston: Little, Brown, 1987), pp. 253–58. All this forced the Senate in 1986 and 1987 to take budget resolutions far more seriously than it had earlier in the decade. The House, lacking comparable resolve, did not tighten its enforcement rules. But any process "self-discipline" was not impressive because the very modest magnitude of the reductions mandated by each year's resolution.

CHAPTER 6

1. White and Wildavsky (1989), p. 558.

2. Barbara Hinckley, *Stability and Change in Congress*, 4th edition (New York: Harper and Row, 1987) explains these norms in detail.

3. James Sundquist, "Needed: A Political Theory for the New Era of Coalition Government in the United States," *Political Science Quarterly* 103:629–30.

4. White and Wildavsky (1989), p. 427.

5. Of the large literature on public choice, one work presenting many of its precepts in an accessible manner is James Buchanan and Richard Wagner, *Democracy in Deficit: The Political Legacy of Lord Keynes* (New York: Academic Press, 1977).

6. A thorough summary of recent Marxist political analysis by American academics can be found in chapter 8 of Martin Carnoy, *The State and Democratic Theory* (Princeton: Princeton University Press, 1984).

7. Buchanan and Wagner, p. 9.

8. Paul E. Peterson and Mark Rom, "Macroeconomic Policymaking: Who Is In Control?" in John E. Chubb and Paul E. Peterson, eds., *Can the Government Govern?* (Washington: Brookings Institution, 1989), p. 178.

9. James Buchanan, "Budgetary Bias in Post-Keynesian Politics: the Erosion and Potential Replacement of Fiscal Norms," in James Buchanan, Charles Rowley, and Robert Tollison, *Deficits* (New York: Basil Blackwell, 1987).

10. Ibid., p. 181.

11. Ibid., p. 183.

12. James O'Connor, *The Fiscal Crisis of the State* (New York: Saint Martin's, 1973).

13. Ibid., p. 9.

14. Ibid., pp. 9–10.

15. Ibid., p. 8.

16. Joseph White and Aaron Wildavsky, "Public Authority and the Public Interest: What the 1980s Budget Battles Tell Us about the American State," *Journal of Theoretical Politics* 1:9.

17. Fred Block, "The Ruling Class Does Not Rule: Notes on the Marxist Theory of the State," *Socialist Revolution* 33:7–8.

18. Two other recent works on Congress elaborate on the importance of intentionality in understanding Congress: Arthur Maass, *Congress and the Common Good* (New York: Basic Books, 1983), and David Vogler and Sidney Waldman, *Congress and Democracy* (Washington: Congressional Quarterly, 1985).

19. On political rationality, see Aaron Wildavsky, "The Political Economy of Efficiency: Cost-Benefit Analysis, Systems Analysis and Program Budgeting," *Public Administration Review* 26:292–310.

Selected Bibliography

Bernstein, Robert A. *Elections, Representation, and Congressional Voting Behavior.* Englewood Cliffs, N.J.: Prentice-Hall, 1989.

Birnbaum, Jeffrey H., and Murray, Alan S. *Showdown at Gucci Gulch.* New York: Random House, 1987.

Blinder, Alan S. *Hard Heads, Soft Hearts.* Reading, Mass.: Addison-Wesley, 1987.

Buchanan, James, and Wagner, Richard. *Democracy in Deficit: The Political Legacy of Lord Keynes.* New York: Academic Press, 1977.

Clausen, Aage. *How Congressmen Decide: A Policy Focus.* New York: St. Martin's Press, 1973.

Collander, Stanley. *Guide to the Federal Budget: Fiscal Year 1987 Edition.* Washington, D.C.: Urban Institute Press, 1986.

Courant, Paul, and Gramlich, Edward. *Federal Budget Deficits: America's Great Consumption Binge.* Englewood Cliffs, N.J.: Prentice-Hall, 1985.

Davidson, Roger. *The Role of the Congressman.* New York: Pegasus, 1969.

Ellwood, John E., and Thurber, James A. "The New Congressional Budget Process: The Hows and Whys of House–Senate Differences." In *Congress Reconsidered,* pp. 188–215. Edited by Lawrence C. Dodd and Bruce I. Oppenheimer. New York: Praeger, 1977.

Fenno, Richard. *Congressmen in Committees.* Boston: Little, Brown, 1973.

———. *Home Style: House Members in Their Districts.* Boston: Little, Brown, 1978.

Fiorina, Morris. *Congress: Keystone of the Washington Establishment.* New Haven: Yale University Press, 1977.

Gilmour, John. *Reconcilable Differences.* Berkeley: University of California Press, 1990.

Greider, William. *The Education of David Stockman and Other Americans.* New York: Dutton, 1982.

Hailstones, Thomas J. *Viewpoints on Supply-Side Economics.* Reston, Va.: Reston Publishing, 1982.

Hinckley, Barbara. *Stability and Change in Congress.* Fourth Edition. New York: Harper and Row, 1987.

Jacobson, Gary. *The Politics of Congressional Elections.* Second Edition. Boston: Little, Brown, 1987.

Kamlet, Mark, Mowery, David C., and Tsai Tsu Zu. "Whom Do You Trust: An Examination of Congressional and Executive Economic Forecasts." *Journal of Management and Policy Analysis* 6:365–84.

Kingdon, John W. *Congressmen's Voting Decisions.* Third Edition. Ann Arbor: University of Michigan Press, 1989.

LeLoup, Lance T. *Budgetary Politics.* Third Edition. Brunswick, Ohio: King's Court Communications, 1986.

_____. "After the Blitz: Reagan and the U.S. Congressional Budget Process." *Legislative Studies Quarterly* 7:321–39.

_____. *The Fiscal Congress.* Westport, Conn.: Greenwood Press, 1980.

Maass, Arthur. *Congress and the Common Good.* New York: Basic Books, 1982.

Matthews, Donald, and Stimson, James A. *Yeas and Nays.* New York: John Wiley and Sons, 1975.

Mayhew, David. *Congress: The Electoral Connection.* New Haven: Yale University Press, 1973.

Miller, W. E., and Shanks, J. M. "Policy Directions and Presidential Leadership: Alternative Interpretations of the 1980 Presidential Election." *British Journal of Political Science* 12:299–356.

Minarik, Joseph J., and Penner, Rudolph G. "Fiscal Choices." In *Challenge to Leadership,* pp. 279–317. Edited by Isabel V. Sawhill. Washington: Urban Institute, 1988.

Moynihan, Daniel Patrick. *Coping: Essays on the Practice of Government.* New York: Random House, 1973.

Musgrave, Richard A., and Musgrave, Peggy B. *Public Finance in Theory and Practice.* Second Edition. New York: McGraw-Hill, 1976.

Palmer, John L. "The Hidden Story of the Deficit." Washington, D.C., 1986. Typescript.

Peterson, Paul E., and Rom, Mark. "Macroeconomic Policymaking: Who Is In Control?" In *Can the Government Govern?,* pp. 139–84. Edited by John E. Chubb and Paul E. Peterson. Washington: Brookings Institution, 1989.

Rauch, Jonathan. "The Fiscal Ice Age." *National Journal,* 10 January 1987, 58–64.

Reischauer, Robert D. "Getting, Using and Misusing Economic Information." In *Making Economic Policy in Congress,* pp. 214–246. Edited by Allen Schick. Washington: American Enterprise Institute, 1983.

Roberts, Paul Craig. *The Supply-Side Revolution.* Cambridge: Harvard University Press, 1984.

Savage, James D. *Balanced Budgets and American Politics.* Ithaca: Cornell University Press, 1988.

Schick, Allen. *The Capacity to Budget.* Washington, D.C.: Urban Institute, 1990.

———, ed. *Crisis in the Budget Process:Exercising Political Choice.* Washington, D.C.: American Enterprise Institute, 1986.

———, ed. *Making Economic Policy in Congress.* Washington, D.C.: American Enterprise Institute, 1983.

———. *Reconciliation and the Congresssional Budget Process.* Washington, D.C.: American Enterprise Institute, 1981.

———. *Congress and Money: Budgeting, Spending and Taxing.* Washington, D.C.: Urban Institute Press, 1980.

Schier, Steven E. *Thinking about the Macroeconomy: The House and Senate Budget Committees in the 1980's.* Monograph Series in Political Science. Washington, D.C.: American Academy of Higher Education, 1986.

———. "The Political Economy of Congressional Budget Voting." Paper presented at the annual meetings of the Northeastern Political Science Association, Boston, 17 November 1986.

Schneider, Jerrold E. *Ideological Coalitions in Congress.* Westport, Conn.: Greenwood Press, 1978.

Shuman, Howard E. *Politics and the Budget.* Second Edition. Englewood Cliffs, N.Y.: Prentice-Hall, 1987.

Smith, Steven S. "New Patterns of Decisionmaking in Congress." In *The New Direction in American Politics,* pp. 203–34. Edited by John E. Chubb and Paul E. Peterson. Washington, D.C.: Brookings Institution, 1985.

Stockman, David. *The Triumph of Politics.* New York: Harper and Row, 1986.

Sundquist, James. "Needed: A Political Theory for the New Era of Coalition Government in the United States." *Political Science Quarterly* 103:629–30.

Weatherford, M. Stephen, and McDonnell, Lorraine M. "The Role of Presidential Ideology in Economic Policymaking." *Policy Studies Journal* 10:691–702.

West, Darrell. *Congress and Economic Policymaking.* Pittsburgh: University of Pittsburgh Press, 1987.

White, Joseph. "What Budgeting Cannot Do: Lessons of Reagan's and Other Years." Washington, D.C., 1986. Typescript.

White, Joseph, and Wildavsky, Aaron. *The Deficit and the Public Interest.* Berkeley: University of California Press, 1989.

———. "Public Authority and the American State: What the 1980s Budget Battles Tell Us about the American State." *Journal of Theoretical Politics* 1:7–31.

———. "How To Fix the Deficit—Really." *Public Interest* 94:3–24.

Wildavsky, Aaron. *The New Politics of the Budgetary Process*. Glenview, Ill.: Scott Foresman, 1988.

――――. "The Political Economy of Efficiency: Cost-Benefit Analysis, Systems Analysis and Program Budgeting." *Public Administration Review* 26:292–310.

INDEX